A handy guidebook
to more than 50 butterfly, skipper,
and moth families

Butterflies

the World　　　　**Alexander B. Klots**

A·Ridge Press Book

BANTAM BOOKS
TORONTO · NEW YORK · LONDON · SYDNEY

Photo Credits

BC Bruce Coleman
John Akester (BC): 83; Ron Austing (BC): 89, 155 (btm.); Jen & Des Bartlett (BC): 8 (btm.), 34, 72 (btm.), 84 (top), 151; S. C. Bisserot (BC): 9 (top), 17 (btm.), 18, 33 (top), 56, 71 (top & btm.), 74 (top & btm.), 101 (btm.), 117, 137 (btm.), 143, 144, 148; Alan Blank (BC): 137 (top), 153 (top); J. M. Burnley (BC): 29; Jane Burton (BC): 22, 26–27 (top), 30, 63, 66, 69 (top & btm.), 86–87, 115, 123, 150, 153 (btm.); B. Brooks (BC): 65 (btm.); J. H. Carmichael, Jr. (BC): 104; B. J. Coates (BC): 33 (btm.), 82; J. A. L. Cooke (BC): 72 (top); D'Arrera (BC): 121, 130 (both); H. N. Darrow (BC): 32 (top & btm.), 99, 111; E. R. Denninger (BC): 9 (btm. left), 11, 23 (top), 45, 78 (btm.), 91, 118; Robert L. Dunne (BC): 92; G. Ernst (BC): 155 (top); M. P. L. Fogden (BC): 28 (btm.), 43, 139 (top); Neville Fox-Davies (BC): 62, 110, 142; David Hughes (BC): 16; G. E. Hyde (BC): 12, 147; Alexander B. Klots: 4, 6, 13, 14, 15 (btm.), 20, 23 (btm.), 26 (btm.), 31 (top & btm.), 39, 44 (top & btm.), 46–47, 50, 53, 55 (btm.), 57, 59 (top), 60, 61, 65 (top), 67, 73, 78–79 (top), 80, 84 (btm.), 94–95, 96, 97, 98, 103 (top), 105, 106 (top), 128, 131, 132; Frank W. Lane (BC): 134; J. Markham (BC): 49, 51, 106 (btm.), 119; A. Muyshondt: 138, 156; D. Overcash (BC): 21, 76, 85, 88, 154; Oxford Scientific Films (BC): 8 (top), 9 (btm. rt.), 17 (top), 24–25, 77; Robert E. Pelham (BC): 28 (top), 47 (top); D. C. Rentz (BC): 42, 52 (left & rt.), 107; K. Roever: 108; E. S. Ross: 41, 55 (top), 81, 103 (btm.), 113, 124, 135, 139 (btm.), 140, 146; J. Shaw (BC): 15 (top), 70, 126 (top), 141, 145, 149, 152; M. W. F. Tweedie (BC): 38, 40, 48, 59 (btm.), 75, 90, 101 (top); L. West (BC): 109, 112, 125, 126 (btm.), 133

Front cover: Orange-tip butterfly, Jane Burton (BC)
Back cover: Irish white prominent moth, S.C. Bisserot (BC)
Title Page: Large Tortoiseshell, G. E. Hyde (BC)
Illustration p. 7: Dennis Prince

BUTTERFLIES OF THE WORLD

A Bantam Book published by arrangement with The Ridge Press, Inc.
Text prepared under the supervision of Laurence Urdang Inc.
Bantam edition-July 1976
2nd printing...April 1983
Designed and produced by The Ridge Press, Inc. All rights reserved.
Copyright © 1976 in all countries of the International Copyright Union
by The Ridge Press, Inc. This book may not be reproduced in whole
or in part, by mimeograph or any other means, without permission.
For information address: The Ridge Press, Inc.,
25 West 43rd Street, New York, N.Y. 10036.

ISBN-0-553-23679-2

Library of Congress Catalog Card Number: 75-42868
Published simultaneously in the United States and Canada.

Contents

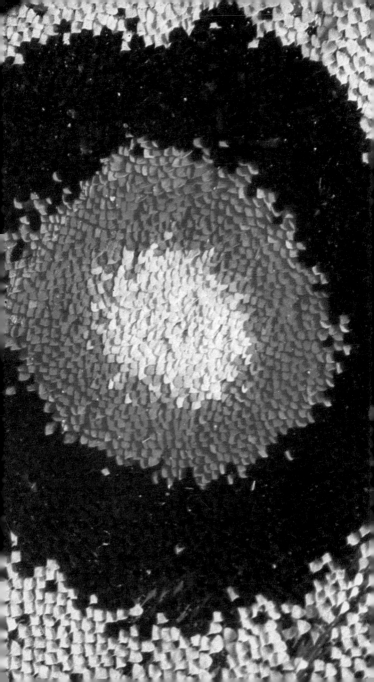

Introduction

Moths, skippers, and butterflies—some of our most common and familiar insects—make up the insect order Lepidoptera. The name of the order comes from two Greek words meaning "scale" and "wing," referring to the tiny, flat scales that cover the wings like shingles and give them their colors and patterns. This second largest order of insects—exceeded only by Coleoptera, the beetles—contains perhaps one hundred thousand different species. There are Lepidoptera from arctic tundras to tropical forests to arid deserts, and in every environment they play a major ecologic part in their relationships with plants and other animals. Their range of size is great—from midget moths, with a wing expanse of only a few millimeters; up to enormous moths and butterflies, expanding nearly three hundred millimeters (over a foot). Some are weak fliers, but others are known to migrate a thousand miles or more, and sometimes even to cross oceans.

Life History

Like most other insects, moths and butterflies go through a metamorphosis involving a decided change of form. Their metamorphosis, called "complete" or "abrupt," involves four distinct stages: egg, larva (or caterpillar), pupa (or chrysalis), and adult. The eggs are small, usually hard-shelled units that can be produced in large numbers and placed by the female where they will have the best chance of survival. In some species the female may produce as many as one or two thousand, which may be laid individually or in groups.

The larva is a relatively simple, long, thin creature whose chief function is to eat, digest, and grow. Its antennae are short, and its eyes are merely two groups of tiny, simple ocelli. It has a pair of strong jaws (mandibles) for grinding great quantities of 5

◀ Wing scales form Parnassius eye-spot

plant matter. Very large silk glands, extending far back into the body, secrete liquid silk that is poured from a spinneret near the mouth and hardens to form a thread. On each of the three segments of the thorax is a pair of short, strong legs; on the abdomen are more (usually five) pairs of fleshy "prolegs." The larva—the nutritive stage of the life cycle—has an enormous and efficient digestive tract.

As the larva grows it sheds its entire outer covering, or molts, a number of times, and each molt forms a new and larger head capsule and integument, shedding the old ones. Many larvae are relatively plain in shape and color, with only sparse hairs, but others, especially those that feed out in the open, show a variety of colors and patterns and may bear dense hairs or spines or strong projections, which have great protective value. Sometimes the larval life may last only a couple of weeks, although it is usually longer, or may extend as long as three years.

When full grown the larva molts for the last time and transforms into a pupa. This is almost inactive, remaining quiet on the exterior. Internally, however, great changes take place as the adult structures develop. The pupa may be formed inside a silk cocoon spun by the larva; a great many are formed in a cell in the ground. Most moth and skipper pupae are quite plain, smooth, and brown. Many butterfly pupae, called "chrysalids," are irregularly shaped and brightly colored, often metallic. **6** These are commonly fixed to a button of silk and hang head

Development Stages of Moths and Butterflies

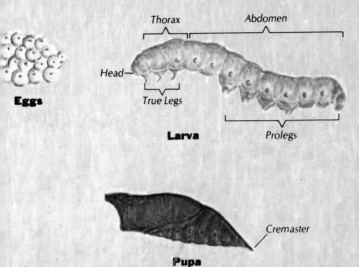

Eggs

Head

Thorax

Abdomen

True Legs

Prolegs

Larva

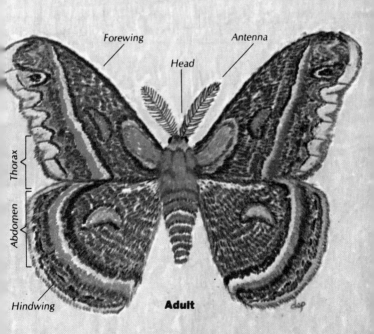

Cremaster

Pupa

Forewing

Head

Antenna

Thorax

Abdomen

Hindwing

Adult

▲ Cabbage White laying egg ▼ Io Moth larvae hatching

▼ Pine Sphinx larva

▼ Newly formed Monarch chrysalis ▼ Monarch fully formed in chrysalis

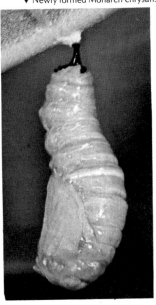 

downward, or are supported by a silk button and girdle around the body. The transformation of the larva into the adult may be accomplished in only a couple of weeks, or may take as much as two or three years, depending on the species and season.

When the adult is fully formed and conditions are right it bursts the pupal shell and crawls out. The adult must hang while its wings, now little, soft pads, expand and its outer structures harden. The adult is very different from the workaday larva from which it grew. Its whole life is oriented toward sensitivity and mobility, enabling it to carry out its primary functions of mating, multiplying, and dispersing its species. Feeding, though important, is secondary. Its two large compound eyes are excellent for detecting motion, the patterns and colors of flowers, and potential mates. Its antennae are usually thickly set with sensory nerve endings for smell and taste. One or two pairs of sensory mouth-parts, the palpi, function similarly. In many groups sensitive taste structures on the soles of the feet detect even minute concentrations of sugars, such as that on flowers, and cause a reflex uncoiling of the proboscis, or tongue. This is usually a long, double tube, coiled beneath the face, through which can be sucked the nectar of flowers, sap, water, or other liquids. The legs are long but strong, with hooks at their tips for a secure hold while perching. At the posterior end of the abdomen are highly modified appendages used in mating and by females for placing and affixing eggs.

The adults of various families differ enormously from each other in nearly every way. The wings may be greatly reduced, or in the females of some groups, may be entirely absent. In many "micro" moths the wings are extremely narrow, with broad **10** fringes of long hair-scales. In some groups the scales are absent,

Monarch emerging from chrysalis ▶

causing large, transparent areas on the wings. The antennae can be very small or widely plumy or long and slender, as most often is the case. The proboscis may be vestigial and useless; such adults cannot feed but must subsist on food stored when they were larvae. Many species can fly but weakly, and then only for short distances. Others, however, have large bodies packed with strong flight muscles, and are capable of sustained flight for hours or days, or of fast darting flight, and even of flying backward. They often have beautifully streamlined wings and bodies.

◀ Hawk Moth, *Hyles* ▼ Plumy antennae of male Promethea Moth

Classification

The classification of the order Lepidoptera is very complex, depending on many technical features. The opinions of authorities differ considerably, but in general the order is divided into three suborders, eighteen superfamilies, and one hundred or more families. A few of the families are very large and contain thousands of species, such as owlet moths (Noctuidae), measuring-worm moths (Geometridae), and pyralid moths (Pyralidae). Other families may consist of only a few species.

Despite their prominence and familiarity, butterflies are merely one superfamily—the Papilionoidea—and skippers, often confused with butterflies, another—the Hesperioidea. They add up to no more than a tenth of the whole order, the other nine-tenths being moths. How can one tell butterflies (and skippers) from moths? This is a common question, to which there is no single, sure answer. Butterflies are day-fliers, but so are many moths. We think of butterflies as having bright colors and of moths as being drab, but many butterflies are dull-colored and many moths are brightly colored and patterned, some of them more so than almost any butterfly. Butterflies have a knob, or club, at the end of each antenna, while the antennae of most moths are either hairlike and tapering, or plumy; but **13**

there are families of moths with clubbed antennae. The majority of moths have a special apparatus for linking together the wings in flight, a task accomplished in butterflies largely by the friction of the overlapping parts. But a great many moths lack this mechanism. There is obviously no simple answer so that we must go on a general consensus when distinguishing butterflies and skippers from moths.

Controls and Enemies

It is inevitable that any group of plant eaters as large and numerous as the Lepidoptera should, in turn, be eaten by a great number and variety of other animals. Frogs, lizards, birds, bats, and other small mammals eat them directly, as do spiders and predatory insects such as praying mantids, ground beetles, ants, wasps, and hornets. Huge numbers, however, are killed by the so-called parasitic wasps and flies, of which there are thousands of species. An adult female of one of these lays her eggs in or on a caterpillar, which is usually of a species on which her own species specializes. The wasp or fly larvae then live inside the caterpillar, gradually consuming it and eventually causing its death. Such parasites are more important in the control of caterpillars than the predators. Many bacteria and viruses also attack the Lepidoptera, sometimes causing vast mortality. Only the enormous reproductive powers of moths, butterflies, and skippers enable them to survive the attacks of so many hostile **14** organisms.

▲ Parasitized Sphinx larva ▼ Praying Mantis eating Alfalfa Butterfly

▼ False eyes protect Sphingid larva, Europe

Defenses

The Lepidoptera cannot physically resist attacks with strong jaws, hard shells, or poison stings as insects of other orders do. They have, however, evolved other means of protection to a high degree of effectiveness. Many make cases in which they live hidden during critical periods. Very important are adaptations of form and color that enable them to escape the notice of or deceive enemies. They have also developed, to a degree that we do not even now fully realize, chemical defenses that either repel or actually poison attackers; and along with these they have developed ways of "advertising" these defenses. Adaptations of these types occur in many other groups of animals, but the effectiveness of Lepidoptera defenses is outstanding.

▲ "Warning" display of a Saturniid, Trinidad ▼ Pupal cell in ground, Sphinx Moth

▲ Puss Moth larva spinning cocoon

Hiding, Shelters, and Cases

The Lepidoptera have evolved many interesting but relatively simple ways for avoiding the notice of enemies or escaping from them. Many moths are extremely flat, like the American copper underwing *(Amphipyra pyramidoides),* and crawl into crevices or under loose bark during the daytime. A good many larvae hide, also. Large numbers of the economically injurious cutworms (Noctuidae) are active only at night and spend the daylight hours buried in surface trash. (Birds such as towhees and song sparrows that scratch vigorously are likely to find many of these.) And many moths with no particular adaptations of form or color merely rest immobile on the undersides of leaves and seem to be quite safe as long as they do not fly. In fact, mere immobility, in itself, is a good defense against sight-hunters.

Some larvae construct shelters of one sort or another where they spend practically all of their lives. It is hard to find a tree or shrub on which the leaves have not been rolled or folded to form simple cases. Sometimes the larva merely eats the soft tissues of the case, and when finished, moves over and makes another one. Other kinds keep the case intact, only leaving it to feed at night. Still others (and these are abundant, especially among the tortricid, olethreutid, and pyralid moths) stitch parts of two or more leaves together to form a commodious case in which they remain during daytime; often these cases are merely enlarged as the larva grows. Some skipper and butterfly larvae also do this, pupating in the case or nest itself or else leaving it and traveling quite a distance to pupate.

A unique type of case is the portable one, almost entirely a specialty of two moth families—the case bearers (Coleophoridae) and the bagworms (Psychidae). The former are small moths, but the bagworm cases often are two to three inches long and elaborately ornamented with bits of twigs or leaves. The larva's first act on leaving the eggshell is to make a tiny case, **19**

continuing to add on to it until it is full grown. One small group of aquatic larvae of the subfamily Nymphulinae make cases of living bits of the aquatic plants on which they feed. Finally, some larvae (especially some of the measuring worms, Geometridae) have the habit of affixing bits of leaves or petals to themselves—a very effective means of masking their identities.

Social Groups and Nests

Quite a number of Lepidoptera are sociable and stay together in groups, chiefly as larvae. None are truly social, living in organized groups like those of ants, bees, and wasps. Rather, the lepidopterous larvae from a single egg mass aggregate together and benefit from being members of a group, especially when they have a special means of protection. Usually, the larvae scatter as they grow older, but in some instances they stay together, often building up sizable webs due to the larval habit of continually spinning out a thread of silk at every move. Tent caterpillars (Malacosoma) and webworms (Hyphantria) are examples of this phenomenon. Some butterflies have the same habit; one Mexican pierid (Eucheira socialis) builds such firm **20** larval nests that they are said to be used by people as flasks.

Bagworm case, New York ▲ Tent Caterpillars and tent ▶

▼ Spinelike chrysalis of Orange Tip

Protective Form and Coloration

Crypsis, or the evolution of form or coloration that enables escape from the notice of predators, is common in Lepidoptera. Not only adults, but leaf-living larvae and butterfly pupae as well are often colored and shaped like leaves. However, it is the adult moths, in particular, that often match the colors and patterns of the bark on which they rest during the daytime. Another major type of camouflage is *disruption,* which disguises the outline of an object by bold and contrasting patches of color and shading. This may be reinforced by unusual shapes and projections, still further changing the outline. The moth, **22** caterpillar, or chrysalis need not resemble any particular thing;

▲ Cryptic Hawk Moth, *Ceratomia* ▼ Disruption, Owlet Moth, *Zale*

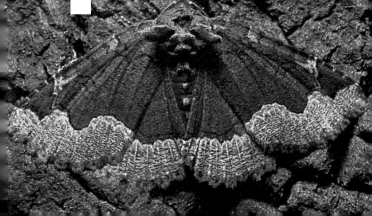

▼ Cryptic moth, Trinidad ▲ Cryptic moth ▼ Cryptic Geometrid, Trinidad

▲ Flowerlike Eucleid

▲ Defense display of Eyed Hawk, Europe ▼ "Bird dropping" Olethreutid, New York

it merely does not look like anything that would prompt a predator to peck at or grab. Other Lepidoptera, especially adult moths and caterpillars, have evolved close resemblances to specific objects, such as dead leaves, broken stems, twigs, thorns, and even bird droppings. Still other Lepidotera can have a cryptic appearance one moment, and then quickly expose something every different. For example, when disturbed, a moth may suddenly reveal a pattern of black and orange or red "flash colors," or expose a pair of enormous eye-spots that have a startling effect. Such adaptations are particularly valuable against daylight-feeding monkeys, birds, and lizards.

▲ Flannel Moth larva, Florida ▼ Slug Caterpillar, *Thosia,* Borneo

Hairs, Spines, and Scales

Often, larvae have long, dense hair—such as the "woolly bear" caterpillars—and it is difficult to realize that there is a conventional caterpillar inside the mass. When disturbed, they often coil into a tight doughnut. Their woolly vesture effectively repels the attackers, for few birds seem to relish them. Other larvae have dense coverings of protruding spines, which also serve as protection from predators. Some moths are covered with a dense mat of long hairs and scales. These scales are often loose, so that when one tries to hold the moth it slips away at the expense of some of its covering. These scales are also useful in escaping from sticky spider webs, which can be an important factor in the survival of the moth. Spiders are among the chief enemies of flying insects, most of which seem to have no protective adaptations against them. **29**

▲ Coiled Buck Moth larva

Chemical Defenses

Many species have evolved a variety of chemical defenses. They can obtain substances, such as the cardenolid heart poisons secreted by plants of the milkweed family, by feeding on plants that are poisonous to other animals. Other Lepidoptera manufacture poisons themselves, such as the cyanides that circulate in the blood of the burnet moths. Often the poisons are on sharp, barbed hairs or spines. Even a single dose of such a poison will make a predator very ill. It has been shown that birds, for example, will quickly learn the appearance of such protected species, and will then leave them alone. To strengthen this effect the protected species have evolved bold, distinctive colors and patterns that are easily remembered and serve as "warning" signals. Such distinctive appearances are called *aposematic,* which is derived from a Greek word meaning "a signal."

▲ Garden Tiger, *Arctia caja*, England ▼ American Garden Tiger larva

▲ Viceroy (mimic) ▼ Monarch (model)

Mimicry

True biological mimicry is based on the evolution of aposematic appearances by chemically protected species. It is of two chief types, named after the men who first worked them out: Batesian mimicry is the strong resemblance of an unprotected, edible species to a protective, aposematic one. Possible predators mistake the harmless mimic for the protected model, and leave it alone. Müllerian mimicry, on the other hand, is the mimicry of **32** one protected species by another, or the convergence on a

▲ Golden Danaid (model) ▼ Female "Eggfly" (mimic)

common appearance of more than one protected species or group. Each is both a mimic and a model for the other. This gives a predator only one, or a few, aposematic appearances to learn and remember. So, at the cost of only one or two individuals, or even of none at all, a species can gain security from predators that have learned, the hard way, to leave it alone. Note the analogy to our own advertising of certain brand names or label patterns—think of all the different kinds of soups that benefit from imitating the distinctive, aposematic, red-and-white can! **33**

Sonic Defenses

Two unusual types of defense mechanisms, based on the detection or production of sound, or both, are found in some of the largest groups of night-flying moths. The moth has a pair of tympanic hearing organs that detect sound waves far above the limits of human audition, but in the range of the "sonar" apparatus of bats, which they use to find and catch their prey. Hearing the bats' sounds, the moth can take evasive action. In addition, large groups of these moths, such as the tiger moths (Arctiidae), can themselves produce sounds in the same supersonic range and thereby temporarily "jam" the bats' mechanism. Since the moths are genuinely protected, their sounds are an aposematic warning to the bats. This was only recently realized when electronic means of detecting and measuring these high-pitched sounds were developed.

Moths, Butterflies, and the Environment

Despite their numbers and complexity, Lepidoptera are surprisingly alike in the all-important matters of foods and feeding. They are nearly all green-plant eaters, concentrating primarily on foliage. The great majority chew up leaves, but many small moth larvae, the so-called leafminers, actually tunnel, or mine, inside leaves, feeding on the soft, juicy tissue. Unlike many insects in other orders, only a tiny minority feed on other animals as parasites or predators. Some bore into fruits, seeds, plant galls, or wood; some are scavengers on dead and decaying plant or animal matter. The adults (some do not feed at all) usually visit flowers for nectar, but many are attracted to sap, juicy carrion, excrement, or rotting fruits.

To the ecologist, moths and butterflies are *primary consumers,* feeding directly on plant matter and transforming this into animal matter. In this they are exceeded by no other land animals, either numerically or quantitatively, and are one of the major ecologic forces. They are also important in the cross-pollination of insect-dependent flowering plants, although secondary to the bees in this. And even the enormous mass of excreta produced by the incalculable numbers of larvae is ecologically important, for it immediately enriches the soil for the next generation of plants. Any farmer or gardener knows the value of domestic animal manure. Does he or she ever consider the value of the fertilizer from all of the caterpillars?

Economic Importance

Inevitably, thousands of species of Lepidoptera, chiefly moths, are injurious to plants valuable to man. These serious insect pests include species that have been brought over from other continents. Once freed from natural controls that kept their numbers down in their homelands, the introduced species can stage spectacular outbreaks. The European gypsy moth *(Lymantria dispar),* corn borer *(Ostrinia nubilalis),* codling moth *(Laspeyresia pomonella),* and cabbage butterfly *(Pieris rapae)* are imported pests in North America. Some examples of home-grown pests are spruce budworms *(Choristoneura fumiferana)* in North America; nun moths *(Lymantria monacha),* green tortrixes *(Tortrix viridana),* and lackeys *(Malacosoma)* are destructive in the Old World. Everywhere the cutworms—larvae of **35** many Noctuidae—cut off, eat and kill seedlings and young garden plants. Leopard moths and coffee borers (Zeuzera) tunnel in the woods of valuable trees. Codling moths and oriental fruit moths (Laspeyresia molesta) spoil fruits, especially apples. Sod webworms (Pyralidae) are serious pests of grasses. Wax moths (Galleria mellonella) do great damage in beehives. In our homes clothes moths (Tineidae) eat woolens and furs, and Indian meal moths (Plodia interpunctella) and Mediterranean flour moths (Ephestia kuhniella) eat stored grains and cereals.

Although the list of destructive Lepidoptera is long, the same order provides man with important benefits. Flower-visiting moths and butterflies are major contributors to the cross-pollination of food and ornamental plants. The silkworm (Bombyx mori) is still important, despite synthetic fibers. Some predatory moth larvae are useful in controlling scale insects (Homoptera) and a few species are valuable for weed control. Other Lepidoptera have served as invaluable research subjects for work in genetics, geographic distribution, adaptation to the environment, and the mechanisms of evolution. Louis Pasteur's work on silkworm diseases led him to his great work on organisms that cause diseases and fermentation. There are also less tangible benefits of Lepidoptera; the beautiful and graceful butterfly has given pleasure to people since the ancient times, and the ephemeral nature of its life has often been depicted in poetry and literature.

Controls by Man

In order to control injurious insects, man has used poisonous insecticides, and still does. But we now realize that enormous damage has been done to the environment by overuse of such nonselective and long-lasting poisons as DDT. Not only do they kill other forms of life, such as birds and fish, but they cause the death of natural enemies of the pests, such as the parasitic wasps and flies that are the chief agents of biological control. We use these parasites for pest control by rearing them in large numbers in laboratories (they are often imported from other regions), and then releasing them. Some interesting techniques are being developed for attracting males of a pest species into traps baited with female sex hormones. Sterile males are then released to mate with females, producing no offspring. Another modern control uses growth or anti-growth hormones of larvae, causing them to develop improperly, or preventing their normal metamorphosis. Such means of control are undoubtedly very expensive, but they are infinitely preferable to the ecologically disastrous overuse of stable insecticides.

Conservation

It is not surprising that because of the enormous environmental changes that people have brought about, some butterfly and moth species have become extinct and many more are threatened. The xerces blue *(Glaucopsyche xerces),* which formerly lived in the San Francisco area, lasted well into the twentieth century but was exterminated by the city's development. The butterflies' vulnerability was caused by their restricted geographic and environmental range. In England, the large copper *(Lycaena dispar)* was extinct by 1848. Drainage of the fenland was at least partly responsible, but overcollecting also played a part. In New Guinea, the collecting of endangered species of the magnificent bird-wing butterflies *(Ornithoptera),* victims of greedy collectors, is prohibited. An historic colony of the Karner blue *(Plebeius melissa samuelis),* near Albany, New York, is threatened by destruction of its special environment. There are some active conservation groups, such as the North American Xerces Society and the Joint Committee for the Conservation of British Insects. Moreover we now realize that when the population of a moth or butterfly is drastically reduced, it is an indication that something is wrong, and environmental change is occurring. **37**

Mandibulate Moths

Family Micropterigidae

For more than a hundred years learned opinions have differed as to whether these small insects are unusual, highly primitive moths or unusual caddisflies of Trichoptera, the essentially aquatic order of insects most closely related to Lepidoptera. These controversial insects resemble moths in that their wings are covered with scales, among other mothlike characteristics. However, the adults have mandibles used to chew food, utterly unlike the proboscis used only for sucking liquids that is one of the most characteristic features of the ''regular'' moths and butterflies. The adults, which fly chiefly during the day in shady places, visit flowers and make use of their jaws to chew pollen. The larvae feed on mosses and liverworts in wet places. New Zealand has perhaps twenty species, and there is a scattering of others throughout the rest of the world. However we may classify them, they are living fossils.

▼ Eriocraniid Moth, New York

Primitive Moths

Family Eriocraniidae

This widespread family is in many ways the most primitive of Lepidoptera. Their hindwings, which are almost as large as their forewings, have a full set of branching veins, all primitive characteristics. These small moths have fuzzy, long-haired heads; a feature often found in other primitive moths. The mouthparts show vestiges of the biting structures characteristic of other insect orders, but also include a short, sucking-type proboscis. The female has a short, piercing ovipositor with which she can insert her eggs in plant tissue. The legless larvae live in large, untidy, blotchy mines in the leaves of trees such as oak, birch, and chestnut. The pupae, formed in the mines, have legs and other appendages free and usable. They also have long, functional jaws used to cut their way out when ready to emerge. Some of the adults are beautiful, brilliantly colored with metallic gold and purple. Scientists are always particularly interested in primitive survivals such as that of these little moths.

◀ Mandibulate Moths, Europe

39

▼ Ghost Moth, *Hepialus humuli*, England

Ghost and Swift Moths

Family Hepialidae

This is a small but worldwide family of medium- to large-sized moths. Among the most primitive of existing Lepidoptera, they have hindwings that are almost as large as their forewings with a nearly complete set of branching veins. Some adults have a wingspread of several inches. The mouthparts are vestigial, and the antennae are small. The large, slowly developing larvae mostly bore in stems, rootstocks, or turf.

In some species the males form dancing swarms at twilight, into which fly females ready for mating—hence the name "ghost moths." They are often brightly colored with pink, green, or metallic silver, particularly in Africa and Australia. They are especially numerous in Australia, where turf-boring larvae of *Oncopera* are pests in grasslands. North American species are mostly uncommon, or at least little collected, but the European *Hepialus humuli* is widespread.

Fairy Moths

Family Adelidae

Fairy moths are part of a small but worldwide family consisting of nearly three hundred species. Although they have a number of primitive characteristics, they definitely belong with the advanced moths, having hindwings smaller than forewings and a reduced venation. The larvae often mine leaves when small, or may live in flowers or seeds. When older they typically make and live in a flat, bean-shaped case. Their common name probably comes from the very light, fast flight of the adults. In some genera the antennae of the males are incredibly long and slender, sometimes four or more times as long as the wings; those of the females are shorter. Many species fly during the daytime and visit flowers to collect nectar. Tiny though they are, some of the species are among the most beautiful and brilliantly colored Lepidoptera. Some have black wings with metallic silver or gold bars or patches. One common species of eastern North America, the maple case bearer, has a bright orange head and deep blue-purple forewings overlaid with peacock green —yet its wing expanse is less than 10 millimeters!

Yucca Moths

Family Prodoxidae

The yucca moths are a small, wholly American family of small moths that have evolved various degrees of relationships with the plants known as yuccas, or Spanish bayonets. In at least one species, the little white yucca borer, the moth and the plant are mutually dependent. The female moth has a special pair of long tentacles on her maxillary palpi. With these she collects a large ball of yucca pollen, carries this to the pistil of the flower, and pollinates it. This enables the plant to form a fruit and seeds, otherwise it could not. The moth also lays an egg in the pistil, from which develops a larva that eats some (but never all) of the seeds. This has been long cited as a classical case of symbiosis, or the mutual dependence of the moth and the plant. The moth, of course, does not "know" what she is doing—she is incapable of "knowing" anything—but merely follows along an instinctive chain of behavior that her species has evolved, just as the yuccas have evolved their dependence on the moths. Other prodoxids are also dependent on the yuccas, but do not perform this act of pollination.

▲ Slug Caterpillar, Borneo

Slug Caterpillar Moths

Family Eucleidae

The moths of this worldwide family are stout-bodied and often quite hairy, with short, strong wings. They have quick, almost buzzing flights. Some have an arresting appearance, with bright green bands or spots on the red-brown wings. The mouthparts are much reduced. The coin- or wafer-shaped eggs are sometimes extremely thin. The larvae are most unusual, both in their difference from those of most Lepidoptera and in their great variety of forms, colors, patterns, and vesture. Taking the family as a whole it is hard to believe that some of the larvae are members of the same family, or are even moth larvae at all. The small head is carried down, almost invisibly tucked in beneath the front segment of the thorax. The legs and prolegs are much reduced, and may not function for walking in the usual way. Instead, the larva glides along by a series of contractions of the lower surface of the body—this is why the larvae are popularly called "slug caterpillars."

A number of genera have rosettes or clusters of sharp, barbed spines along their sides. These have a painful nettling effect in the skin or mouth of an animal that grasps or touches one of the **43**

◀ Yucca Moths in Yucca flower

Prolimacodes larva ▲ Hag Moth larva ▼ Saddleback, *Sibine stimulea* ▶

larvae, and are an effective protective mechanism. In other genera, however, not only the stinging spines, but practically all other vesture as well have been lost through evolution, and the larvae are smooth. Most eucleid larvae are subject to little predation, but are often parasitized by small braconid wasps that hunt by scent, rather than by sight.

The most unusual larval types are well represented in North America. The larva of the hag moth *(Phobetron pithecium)* is a dull reddish brown, covered with very short hairs. From the sides of the body protrude several pairs of irregular, twisted outgrowths, which are covered with stinging hairs. Its resemblance to a bit of curled, dead leaf is striking. When it spins its oval cocoon the larval outgrowths are transferred to the cocoon, providing a similar kind of protection.

44   Other more "normal" larvae have long, thin bodies bearing a

number of short-spined hornlike projections. These, too, often have stinging spines, and many of them signal their protection by their bright, revealing colors and patterns. The larvae of *Adoneta* and *Euclea* are of this general type, and those of the Asian genus *Thosia* are outstanding examples. The larvae of *Sisyrosea* are extremely flat and lie close to the surface of a leaf; their flatness is enhanced by fringes of spiny projections along their sides. They look as uncaterpillarlike as a caterpillar could. Exceedingly different from these are the smooth larvae of *Prolimacodes* that are high and boxlike. Individuals can vary greatly in their coloration: some are green with a brown back, others are green with a yellow and brown blotched back, and still others are yellow with a brown and green back. These and other cryptic eucleid larvae have an amazing resemblance to protruding galls found on the leaves of their foodplants. **45**

Flannel Moths

Family Megalopygidae

In this small, entirely New World family there are a few North American species and many more in the tropics. The stout-bodied moths have dense hair and deep, soft, flannel-like scaling. The larvae are usually buried in long hairs, but beneath the hairs are sharp spines that produce a painful sting. Some large, brown tropical larvae have even been known to cause hospitalization for the unfortunate who happens to brush against one of them. The larvae have extra pairs of vestigial prolegs ahead and behind the usual abdominal ones. The hard, oval cocoons have a neat, hinged lid that opens outwardly at the end where the moth emerges. Here, the stinging spines that once belonged to the larva form a mass that effectively discourages small animals from trying to open the lid and get to the pupa. Parasitic wasps, undeterred by the protective structures, are the chief means of control.

▼ Lacey's Flannel Moth ▲ Flannel Moth

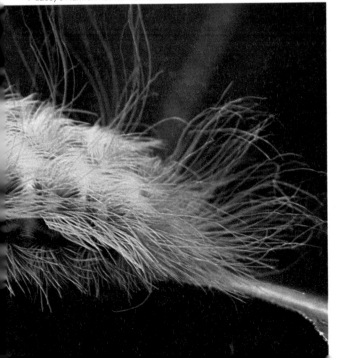

Burnets and Foresters

Family Zygaenidae

The zygaenids are a small but widespread family of brightly colored, day-flying moths that are highly protected from predators by a variety of powerful toxins. The burnets, often abundant, have brilliant red, white, and metallic blue or green patterns, making them conspicuous when flying or visiting flowers. The foresters are plainer. Burnets are especially abundant in Europe where the species vary both individually and geographically. These variations make them popular with collectors. Some species are protected by their ability to carry in their blood extremely poisonous hydrocyanic acid, as well as acetylcholine, histamine, and other toxins. Since their appearance is easily remembered, they are primary examples of aposematism, the evolution of distinctive warning colors and actions by genuinely protected animals, and they are mimicked by other groups of moths. The zygaenids pose a peculiar problem to collectors since they are immune to conventional cyanide killing agents and must be killed by other methods. The New World species, sometimes classified in this family, are separated as the family Pyromorphidae.

▲ Burnet Moths, *Zygaena*, Europe ▶

Pyromorphid Moths

Family Pyromorphidae

These moths are the New World counterparts of the zygaenids, to which they are closely related. Like the zygaenids, they are conspicuous, day-flying flower-visitors, and are highly protected by internal secretions in the blood. When roughly handled they bleed freely at body and leg joints, exposing the attacker to a dose of their toxins. It has been shown that birds, lizards, and even praying mantids are capable of learning to leave them alone. Their resemblance to various species of day-flying, flower-visiting beetles of the family *Lycidae* is striking. These beetles are also highly protected and almost immune from most predators, so that this is a classic case of Müllerian mimicry: because of their mutual resemblances, the beetles and the moths reinforce each other's effects. One type of pyromorphid, such as *Sereda constans,* has forewings that are orange with black tips. It visits flowers along with a similar-looking protected lycid, *Lycus fernandezi.* Other pyromorphids and lycid counterparts have scarlet and black, or steely blue forewings. Protected moths and beetles of other families also enter into Müllerian mimicry relationships.

Clothes and Scavenger Moths
Family Tineidae

This is a worldwide family of scavengers, whose larvae usually make crude, portable cases and can consume everything from decaying vegetation, fungi, and lichens to the debris in bird and animal nests and bat caves. It is quite to be expected that in a family with these food habits some species would invade our homes and develop the habit of eating feathers and animal fibers such as woolens, silks, and furs. The most common species is the pale yellow *Tineola bisselliella*. However, the clothes moths have largely ceased to be the pests that they once were due to effective repellents and insecticides, increased dry-cleaning, and synthetic fibers. The carpet beetles *(Anthrenus)* probably do more damage than the clothes moths but the moths, which are really becoming quite rare, traditionally get the blame. Some tineids are pests on stored foods and in granaries.

The adults are small and rough-haired, and can be shades of gray, brown, black, or white. Some have small metallic markings. They are narrow-winged; few have a wing expanse of more than a half-inch.

◄ *Sereda constans*, Arizona ▲ Adult Clothes Moth

▲ Bagworm case and pupal shell ▲ Emerged Bagworm Moth

Bagworm Moths

Family Psychidae

This rather small but worldwide family is best known for the cases the larvae spin around themselves almost from the moment of hatching from the egg. These they never leave, carrying them wherever they go, and of course, enlarging them as they grow. (In this they are analogous to the caddisflies of the related order Trichoptera.) The cases are embellished with all sorts of objects such as dead leaves or twigs. In many species the case shows a distinctive shape and style of ornamentation. Those of some of the larger tropical species exceed four inches in length, but those of small species may be only a half-inch.

Along with this has evolved a most extreme degeneration of the adult female, who is wingless and never feeds. She may be, in fact, little more than a crawling sac of massive ovaries and other reproductive organs. Sometimes she never even leaves her pupal shell, let alone the case. Males are attracted to her by scent, fertilizing her hundreds or thousands of eggs. When these hatch, the larvae crawl out of the mother's case and set to work **52** making their own cases in the same or nearby trees or shrubs.

Narrow-winged Leaf Miners

Families Gracillariidae, Lyonetiidae, and others

Quite a number of moth families have evolved to be extremely small, with wing expanses from only three to ten millimeters, a feature that enables the larva to complete its entire development mining in the interior of a leaf. In many instances the pupa is formed in the mine as well. The larvae of many leaf miners have become highly specialized for their lives of burrowing in the soft, wet inner tissues of the leaf. Through evolution the legs often have been partly or entirely lost and the jaws transformed into a pair of forward-thrusting shears. The larvae may also be greatly flattened. To the ecologist, leaf mining is a highly specialized "niche," or way of making a living in a particular environment. Insects of other orders also mine in leaves. The mines of each species are often characteristic in shape and size, and each will mine only in the leaves of a particular species, or group, of plants. Often it is easier to identify the species by its mine than by the insect itself. Many of the adults have exceedingly narrow wings bearing long hair-scale fringes on the margins. Some have beautiful brilliant gold, silver, or copper markings, but due to their minute size most people are unaware of their existence.

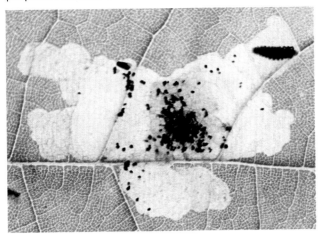

▲ Gracillariid larva in its leaf mine

Wasp, or Clearwing, Moths

Family Sesiidae

The moths of this almost worldwide family have distinctive narrow forewings and wider hindwings, which are sometimes partly transparent. They are often brightly colored with yellow, orange, or red wing markings and bands along the bodies. The hindlegs are usually thickly scaled and marked with yellow or orange. All of this adds up to a very good mimicry of wasps and hornets—insects that are notoriously protected by their stings, and advertise it. Most of the moths fly during the daytime visiting flowers, and there can be no doubt that they derive much protection from their resemblance to wasps. The very large European hornet moth *(Aegeria apiformis)*, whose larvae bore in the trunks and roots of poplar and willow trees, is a particularly impressive mimic of large hornets. The larvae are slow-growing borers in twigs, stems, or rootstocks of a variety of plants. The peach tree borer *(Sanninoidea exitiosa)* and the currant borer *(Trochilium tipuliformis)* can be serious pests.

Ermine and Calico Moths

Family Yponomeutidae

This medium-sized family of small moths (very few have a wingspread more than one and a half inches) has at least a few representatives almost everywhere, with many in tropical regions. Some are rather plain, such as the European ermine moth *(Yponomeuta padella)*, which has white forewings marked with black dots. Its larvae live gregariously in webs on shrubs and fruit trees. The North American calico moth *(Atteva punctella)*, however, is brilliantly colored. Its larvae live in webs on ailanthus (tree of heaven), and the species has extended its range with the spread of this imported tree. Species of the widespread genus *Cerostoma* have not only bold, bright patterns but strongly hooked forewing tips. At rest, the moth looks very unmothlike. The larvae feed on honeysuckle. A number of tropical and subtropical species make extraordinary open lacework cocoons that extend from twig or treetrunk on long, hairlike, but very **54** tough stalks, which may discourage investigating ants.

▲ Clearwing Moth ▼ Calico Moth

Carpenter and Goat Moths

Family Cossidae

This is a small but worldwide family of medium- to very large-sized moths. The adults are often woolly and have narrow wings patterned with small scrawls or dots. Their abdomens are enormous. The Australian *Xyleutes boisduvalii* has a wingspread up to ten inches and an abdomen said to be "as large as a small banana." The wing venation and other structures are quite primitive. Females have been known to lay several thousand eggs. The stout larvae bore in stems, rootstocks, or the roots of trees, or in turf. Due, perhaps, to the poor nutritional quality of wood, some must spend three or more years in the larval stage. Needless to say, the large species can do great damage by their boring in forest, fruit, or shade trees. The European goat moth *(Cossus cossus)*—so-called because the larvae have a "goaty" smell—has even been known to bore in seasoned wood. The European leopard moth *(Zeuzera pyrina)*, introduced into North America, is a well-known pest. In other regions the white borer *(Z. coffeae)* is a pest in coffee trees.

▼ *Cenopis alisellana*

Leaf Roller Moths

Family Tortricidae

This is a large, worldwide family of small-sized moths; few have wing expanses of more than an inch. The straight-ended fore-wings are sometimes brightly colored and patterned. When at rest the moths hold their wings back flat, covering the abdomen. Some have the margins of the forewings doubly curved, causing a bell-shaped outline. The larvae feed on a variety of trees, shrubs, and other plants, usually folding or webbing one or more leaves together. The green *Tortrix viridana* of Europe can be a serious pest on oak trees, defoliating large areas of wood-land. The spruce budworm *(Choristoneura fumiferana)* has been stigmatized as the most serious forest pest of North Ameri-ca, its native habitat. The closely related *C. pini* is brick red and feeds on pines. The larvae of *Acleris minuta* even damage the periodically submerged shrub, cranberry. The damage done by this family is out of proportion to the small size of the individual moths.

◄ Carpenter Moth

Olethreutid Moths

Family Olethreutidae

These small moths are closely related to the Tortricidae. They exist in every area where moths can survive, numbering many thousands of species in the world. Like tortricids they hold their straight-ended wings back over the abdomen. Perhaps the best-known olethreutid is the bronzy-brown codling moth *(Laspeyresia pomonella)*, the worst pest of apples. It is a native of Europe, but has spread almost everywhere. Its larvae are the all too well known "worms" found in apples and occasionally in pears and other fruits. First generation larvae enter the apple blossom, but second generation ones bore into older fruit from the side. Another serious fruit pest is the oriental fruit moth *(Laspeyresia molesta)*, imported into North America from Japan. Its larvae bore in stone fruits, especially peaches. Other species bore in soft fruits, nuts, acorns, flowers, and buds. The majority, however, web and tie together leaves with silk and feed on them. Some even cause galls in stems and twigs. A most versatile family!

Pyralid Moths

Family Pyralidae

The pyralids are the third largest family of the order, although they are sometimes divided by authorities into a number of families. The majority are slender and long-legged, with wing expanses from one-quarter inch to three inches. There is a pair of tympanic hearing organs at the base of the abdomen. Most of the moths are rather dull looking, but some have bright, contrasting patterns of silvery or satiny stripes or bright metallic spots. The majority fly at night or dusk but some, such as the polka dot pyralid *(Pyrausta funebris)*, are diurnal. The moths mostly feed on leaves, lichens, or grass, or bore in stems. Many of the species are abundant, having great ecological influence.

The subfamily Nymphulinae is especially interesting. Most members have adapted to life in fresh water, existing in flowing streams and still lakes—the only Lepidoptera group of considerable size to do this. The larvae bore in stems of aquatic plants,

▲ Codling Moth ▼ Grass Moth, *Chrysoteuchia*, England

make and inhabit cases incorporating living bits of plants, or construct webs attached to rocks and feed on debris. They have special tracheal gills with which they respire. Yet, the adult moths appear to be perfectly normal, many with delicate colors and patterns.

The grass moths (subfamily Crambinae) include species called sod webworms that feed on grasses and often live in turf. Some are distinct lawn, golf course, or meadow pests, and others are serious pests of rice, sugarcane, and corn (maize). The tropics are particularly rich in species. Some adults are attractive, with silvery stripes along the forewings, or bold bands of orange on satiny white.

One small subfamily, the Galleriinae, scavenge in the nests of bees; and wax moths *(Galleria mellonella)* can be pests in honeybee hives. Members of the subfamily Pyraline are scaven-

gers in decaying vegetation or stored cereals, often invading houses, factories, or grain elevators. Some genera of the Phycitinae, another subfamily, do this, too, and may be household or industrial pests, although most phycitines are leaf folders or crumplers. One group, the genus *Cactoblastis*, bore into the succulent stems of cacti. *Cactoblastis cactorum* has been beneficial to man, for it carries a disease of cacti. Introduced into Australia, where imported cacti had invaded enormous areas of valuable rangeland, it spread the disease and brought the spiny weeds under control.

The most infamous pyralid is the European corn borer *(Ostrinia nubilalis)*. Introduced into North America, it threatened to devastate the all-important corn (maize) crop. It has been brought under partial control by parasites and ecological methods of crop management, but is still an ever-present threat. **61**

Polka Dot Pyralid ▲ Grass Moth, *Argyria*, Connecticut ▲

Feather, or Plume, Winged Moths

Family Pterophoridae

The adults of this small, unusual, family are slender-bodied, long-legged, and quite fragile, shedding hairs, scales and legs at the slightest touch. The wings are usually deeply cleft into two or three plumes, all with long fringes. At rest, the wings are usually narrowly rolled or folded, and held out sideways. The larvae are somewhat bristly or sparsely hairy. Some have hollow, glandular hairs that secrete at their tips droplets of a very sticky liquid. It has been observed that minute parasitic wasps, which had undoubtedly approached a larva to lay eggs in it, have been trapped in these droplets. Secretions of this kind are well known in such plants as sundews, bog plants that catch their small insect prey in this way. Among moths, however, protection against parasites by Tanglefoot appears to be unique to the feather wings. The larvae feed on a variety of herbaceous plants and a few shrubs or vines, sometimes boring in the stem and eating the leaves afterward. One species is a minor grape pest.

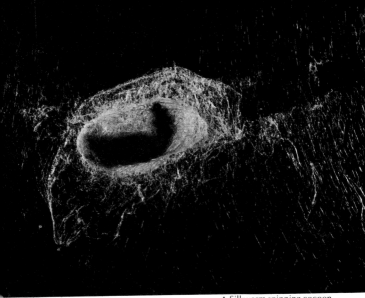

▲ Silkworm spinning cocoon

Silkworm

Bombyx mori

For practical purposes, the silkworm moth is the family Bombycidae, for the few other species are widely scattered and of little interest here. The silkworm has been cultivated in China since the eighteenth century B.C. It is quite unable to maintain itself in nature. The smooth, whitish caterpillar has a short horn on the eighth abdominal segment. It feeds on mulberry leaves, which are grown specifically for this purpose. The cocoon has a tight inner shell that is surrounded by the dense mass of a single, intertwined thread of silk, either white or yellow, depending on the genetic strain. Unreeling this thread can be a difficult task. The adult flies little, if at all.

At one time silk culture was extremely important in many parts of Europe and in the American colonies. In Connecticut, for example, more than $200,000 worth was produced annually. In recent years, however, the demand for silk has dropped sharply, largely because of the many synthetic fibers now available. But we are in debt to the silkworm for more than silk—Louis Pasteur's investigations of a silkworm disease, pebrine, led to some of his pioneering discoveries in bacteriology.

Tent Caterpillars, Lappets, and Eggars

Family Lasiocampidae

At least one or more species of the genus *Malacosoma* is common to abundant almost anywhere in Europe, temperate Asia, and North America. The moths are stout-bodied with short wings. They have reduced mouthparts, and so cannot feed. They lay their eggs in cylindrical masses around twigs, and cover them with a varnish that acts as protection during the winter. Many of the caterpillars are quite hairy and brightly colored and marked. Few birds relish them, but the North American cuckoo is said to be an exception.

"Tent caterpillar" may be a somewhat misleading name. Although the caterpillars of most of the species live gregariously in webs, or tents, to which they return after feeding, some species, such as the forest tent caterpillar *(M. disstria)*, do not make tents at all. Other gregarious so-called webworms, such as some of the arctiids, are often miscalled tent caterpillars. Both the European lackey *(M. neustria)* and the North American *M. americanum* may do considerable damage to fruit trees, and particularly in western North America, some species may defoliate large areas of forest. It was once recommended that the overwintering egg masses be collected and burned, but because many of the eggs are parasitized by minute wasps, this practice defeats its purpose by killing the parasites. Only when the caterpillars are damaging valuable trees should they be controlled with insecticides.

The North American lappet moths, such as those of the genus *Tolype*, are densely hairy. When one of these moths is poked or pinched it often "plays possum," falling on its side with its

▲ Tent Caterpillars on tent ▼ Tent Caterpillar egg mass

wings above its back. Moths of a few other groups have the same defense reaction. Sometimes this may be merely to display an unpalatable hairiness; but in some tiger moths (Arctiidae) it may signal a genuine chemical defense—even a toxic one. Some of the very hairy caterpillars of the European eggar moths, such as the red eggar (*Macrothylacia rubi*) and the oak eggar (*Lasiocampa quercus*) are very brightly and aposematically colored. They are well protected by nettling spines, which causes a severe skin rash in many people.

▲ Oak Eggars mating, England

▲ Hickory Horned Devil.

Regal Moths
Family Citheroniidae

The medium to very large moths of this small, wholly American family are allied to the saturniids. Some are exceedingly striking, their long wings being maroon red, pink, brown, or yellow with contrasting markings. The pupa is formed in a cell in the ground, with no cocoon. The caterpillars of some of the large species are particularly impressive, having large dorsal horns. The most striking is that of the regal moth (*Citheronia regalis*) known as the hickory horned devil. It is a fearsome-looking creature, and most people will not be convinced that it harms nothing but the leaves it eats. The yellow emperor (*Eacles imperialis*) is equally large, its yellow wings bearing many rosy-red marks. In *Anisota,* a genus of smaller species, the rosy maple moth (*A. rubicunda*) is straw yellow with bright pink bands. Its larva, the pink striped mapleworm, is sometimes harmful. So are the larvae of the orange striped oakworm (*A. senatoria),* which have been known to defoliate considerable areas of oak woods. In the New World tropics even larger, more striking species occur.

Giant Silkworm and Emperor Moths

Family Saturniidae

Although this is a small family numerically, it is one of the most widely known. Every continent has species well known for their large size, striking patterns, and unusual wing shapes. The largest are the enormous *Attacus atlas* and *Coscinoscera hercules* of the Indo-Australian regions, with wing expanses up to twelve inches; *hercules* has very broad wings, giving it a greater wing area than a pigeon. The moths have lost their functional mouthparts and so must live on foods stored when they were caterpillars. Both sexes have plumy antennae, those of the males being much wider. The caterpillars are stout-bodied, with a number of fleshy, often brightly colored tubercles. Some have many bristly, and perhaps nettling, spines. In all but one small group, the pupa is formed in a cocoon. Dense and strong, it is commonly fastened to a branch or twig, perhaps with leaves for camouflage. In some genera the adult moths have "cocoon cutters," a pair of small blades located at the forewing bases, which enable them to get out of the cocoon.

What we might call the "Atlas type" (*Attacus* and its relatives) is widespread but most common in the Asiatic and New World tropical regions. In this group, each wing has a large windowed area, transparent because the scales are missing. These are especially large in such Mexican species as *Rothschildia orizaba*. North America has a number of species of this general group, including the cecropia moth (*Platysamia cecropia*) and its relatives. The promethea moth (*Callosamia promethea*) and the very large polyphemus moth (*Antheraea polyphemus*) are common. The big, smooth-skinned caterpillars have especially

▲ Emperor Moth, Europe ▼ Atlas Moth, Asia

large red or yellow tubercles, but they are surprisingly difficult to discern among foliage. One lepidopterist put thirty large cecropia caterpillars in a small apple tree; a few hours later he could pick out only a few. Then he systematically went over every single leaf and twig—and found them all!

The broad, plumy antennae of the males have a very large surface area covered with sensory cells. With these they can scent receptive females, even miles away. The mating flights of promethea are at times very noticeable, since the males seek the females only in the afternoon, and may fly by the dozens around a newly emerged female, even in bright sunshine. The mating flights of the closely related angulifera moth (Callosamia angulifera), which can hybridize with promethea, take place in late evening and after dark.

The North American io moth (Automeris io), a northern representative of a sizable tropical group, has large eyelike spots on the hindwings. The resting moth hides these but exposes them suddenly when disturbed. (The big Antheraea polyphemus, which has close relatives in the Old World, has similar hindwing eyespots.) The caterpillars of this group are brightly colored or elaborately ornamented and bear many sharp, painfully stinging spines. Their distinctive appearances have an aposematic, or "warning," effect.

▲ Ailanthus Moth ▼ *Antheraea paphia*, India

▼ Io Moth displaying ▲ Emperor larva, *S. pavonia*

One group of the saturniids has tails, sometimes very long and graceful, on the hindwings. In some small African species, the tails are longer than the rest of the moth. The Madagascan *Argema mittrei*, a very large, long-tailed species, spins unusual metallic-looking, silvery cocoons. The North American luna moth *(Actias luna)* is one of the most beautiful, being a delicate, pale, lime green when fresh.

Europe has few saturniids, but both the emperor *(Saturnia pavonia)* and the great peacock *(S. pyri)* are common. It was with the latter that the great naturalist Jean Henri Fabre made one of his classic experiments, demonstrating the female's ability to attract males, even from miles away, with the scent she

gives off when she is ready to mate.

Many attempts have been made to take advantage of the copious silk production of saturniids. Silks such as "tussore" are obtained from some Asiatic *Antheraea* in a small way; but in most species the difficulty of unreeling the silk thread from the cocoon makes it an unprofitable venture. At one time the Chinese ailanthus moth *(Samia cynthia)* together with its foodplant, ailanthus, was widely introduced into the United States for silk culture. The boom died out, but both the moth and the tree have survived. Curiously, both do extremely well in highly polluted urban environments where the native saturniids are dying out.

73

▲ Luna Moth, *Actias luna*

Brahmaeid Moths

Family Brahmaeidae

The brahmaeids are a small family of mostly large moths that occur in Africa and across southern Asia to China and Japan, in generally temperate regions. The moths' wings have complicated patterns, and the antennae are narrow and plumy in both males and females. Unlike the giant silkworm moths (Saturniidae), the brahmaeids have a definite proboscis and longer palpi (although it is believed that they do not feed). Their flight is strong and powerful, and they come readily to lights at night.

▲ Brahmaeid larva ▼ Owl Moth, *Brahmaea japonica*

▲ European Currant Moth

Spanworm Moths and Loopers

Family Geometridae

The name Geometridae means "earth measurers," a reference to the characteristic looping gait of the caterpillars, also called "inchworms." The adults of some groups are called "carpets," "waves," or "pugs." This is the second largest family of the order, containing many thousands of species, some of which exist in the far arctic or on high mountaintops. In all but a few species, the larvae have lost most of the abdominal prolegs, and the last pair of these has moved back, close to the rearmost pair. They therefore have legs only at or near the ends. The larvae are often very slender and flexible. Practically all are foliage eaters. **75**

▲ Geometrid larva on Black-eyed Susan flower

▼Geometrid Moth, Jamaica

The pupae are formed in a cell in the ground or in a loose cocoon among leaves or trash.

The caterpillars have evolved a great many camouflaging characteristics. They are slender, like twigs, and many are various shades of brown with cross lines and bumps like the nodes and small buds on twigs. Others are green and lie along the midribs of leaves, or eat away much of a leaf, leave the midrib or a strong vein projecting, and then lie along this. The twig mimics often rest holding on by only the rear legs, with the body and head projecting straight outward. They often spin a strong silk thread that supports the head and eases the strain of holding on by the rear legs alone. Many pine-feeding species have lengthwise green stripes along their body, so that they are almost indistinguishable when they lie among pine needles. Still other larvae fasten bits of leaves or flower petals to their bodies for camouflage.

77

▲ Geometrid, *Lytrosis unitaria* ▼ Geometrid larva looping

A good many species are sometimes severe pests, mostly on trees. The spanworms *(Ennomos magnarius* and *subsignarius)* and the spring and fall cankerworms *(Palaeacrita* and *Alsophila)* are North American examples. In Europe the winter moth *(Operophtera brumata)* and some *Erannis* are similar pests. They may defoliate considerable areas of woodland, weakening the trees and retarding their growth. Cultivated trees and shrubs, from apple and plum to gooseberry and raspberry, are often damaged. (Incidentally, the cankerworms are among a small number of geometrids in which the females are wingless.)

The moths usually have broad, somewhat angular wings and relatively small bodies. Most fly at night and rest during the day, with the wings out flat at the sides, closely pressed to the surface on which they are resting. It is then that they are most vulnerable to attack by birds, but the great majority are cryptically colored and patterned. Often they match their backgrounds almost perfectly, orienting themselves so that their markings continue and blend in with those of the bark. A good many species, including one subfamily, are green and thus well protected among foliage. **79**

These species have a true green pigment in the scales, almost unique in the order. Still other species have a boldly disruptive camouflage that effectively "breaks up" their outlines.

However, not all geometrids are cryptic, for some, like the European currant moth *(Abraxas grossulariata),* are inedible or poisonous. Such species generally have very bright, conspicuous warning appearances, and in keeping with this, make little or no attempt to hide. They will often take a position on the upper surface of a leaf and remain there all day, quite unharmed. The larvae and pupae are also brightly aposematic.

The English peppered moth *(Biston betularia)* has been intensively studied as the best-known example of "industrial melanism." In and around heavily industrial cities, where the air has been badly polluted for a century and a half and has deposited sooty residues on everything, treetrunks that were once light-colored and variegated with lichens have become blackish. Before the age of pollution this moth had a light gray, grizzled pattern that matched the clean bark. Now, in polluted areas the species has changed and is nearly all dark, due to natural selection by moth-eating birds. But in unpolluted areas the species has remained predominantly light. Related geometrids and other moths in both Europe and North America show **80** the same sort of change.

Disruptive crypsis, *Euchlaena* ▲ *Uranidia* ▶

Uranias

Family Uraniidae

This small tropical family exists in the Old and New Worlds, and is famous because of the beauty and unusual habits of its larger species. The large Madagascar urania (*Chrysiridia madagascarensis*) has been called the most beautiful of living things, exceeding even the brilliant hummingbirds and sunbirds. Its black pattern is interspersed with bands of iridescent green, shading to orange and orange-red. On the hindwings are long, graceful tails edged in white. Its glowing colors shift to different hues with every slight change in the angle of view. These are structural colors, caused by a series of thin, overlapping films in the body of each scale. The films are submicroscopic in thick-

ness, but their presence was calculated about fifty years ago by a Cornell University physical chemist. Recently they have been photographed with the help of the scanning electron microscope, thus verifying their existence. A common example of such thin-film colors is the rainbow effect of oil film on water. The shifting and changing color effect is caused by the curvature of each uraniid scale.

The large tropical American species of *Uranidia* are black with iridescent green bands and a long tail on each hindwing. They are strong, fast, day-fliers; some have been observed migrating by the thousands, passing overhead continuously for an entire day. The reasons for such migrations are not understood. In the Indo-Australian region some species of *Alcidis* are well-known day-fliers with iridescent blue to green bands and shorter tails than the New World uraniids. Most curiously, one of these is mimicked by a swallowtail butterfly *(Papilio laglazei)* in New Guinea. The *Alcidis* is common and widespread, while the *Papilio* is rare. This would seem to indicate that the *Alcidis* is the protected model and the *Papilio* a Batesian mimic, since it is almost an axiom that such mimics are not as common as their models. However, the *Papilio* may be protected, in which case this would be a case of Müllerian mimicry. Perhaps the *Papilio* is not as rare as it seems to be.

▲ *Alcidis agathyrsus,* New Guinea
Death's Head Hawk, *Acherontia atropos,* Europe ▶

Hawk Moths and Sphinx Caterpillars

Family Sphingidae

The hawk moths make up a worldwide family of about a thousand species, and are well represented in all continents. They are great favorites with collectors and students. The moths have relatively large bodies and powerful wing muscles. With their large abdomens tapering to a point at the rear, they are often beautifully streamlined. Small species have a wing expanse of no more than an inch and a quarter, while the wings of larger species expand more than eight inches, and are very impressive. The hindwings are much smaller than the forewings, the latter giving most of the flight power. The antennae are thick and prominent. In some groups the adults never feed, as the tongue is reduced and nonfunctional. In the majority,

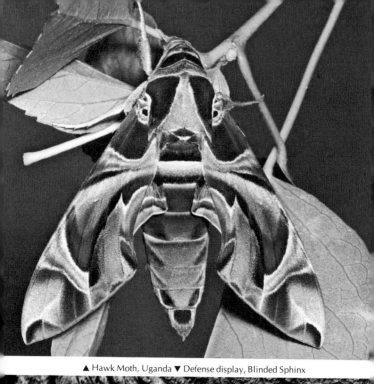

▲ Hawk Moth, Uganda ▼ Defense display, Blinded Sphinx

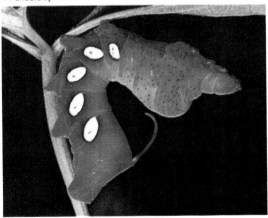

however, the tongue is very long, sometimes more than twice the length of the body, and when not in use is coiled beneath the face. When uncoiled it can be thrust deep into the hearts of even extremely long, tubular flowers. The moth does this while hovering in front of the flower, sustaining itself with exceedingly fast, powerful wingbeats. The moths are often important in the pollination of flowers. Some flowering plants—members of the morning glory family and the orchids—seem to be dependent upon particular hawk moths for cross-pollination.

The sphingids are one of the most attractive groups of Lepidoptera. The species differ greatly in appearance—some are dull gray or brown, others are brilliantly colored and boldly patterned with combinations of green, yellow, orange, and even pink or blue on the hindwings. One group has large orange, yellow, or pink spots along the sides of the abdomen.

During the daytime most of the species hang on foliage or bark and fly at dusk, night, or dawn. Their cryptic colors and patterns, which are often disruptive, keep them fairly safe. But some species, even large ones, fly actively even during the hottest days and rely on their power and speed to escape attackers. In one widespread group, including various species of the genus *Smerinthus,* each hindwing bears a prominent, bright eyespot. When a resting individual is disturbed it makes no attempt to flee. Instead, it stretches the forewings forward, **85**

exposing the eyespots, and then rocks back and forth. This "startle" mechanism must be effective against attackers or it never would have evolved.

The moths of many species are strongly attracted to lights, especially to fluorescent ones and the black lights used by collectors. The moths are, of course, mostly attracted to fragrant, tubular flowers such as petunia, honeysuckle, and nicotiana. In fact, people often plant beds of these flowers just to attract the moths.

A considerable number of the smaller species are day fliers, tirelessly visiting flowers from dawn to dusk. Of these, the widespread genus *Macroglossum* extends across Europe and Asia to Australia. *Macroglossum stellatarum* is common in

▲ Broad Bordered Bee Hawk, England

Europe but reaches Great Britain only by migration. In flight it makes a high-pitched hum that is barely audible to humans. The sizable North American genus *Hemaris* and the Australian *Cephenodes* have nearly transparent dark-bordered wings. When formed in the pupa the wings are fully scaled, but most scales are shed soon after the moth's emergence. Many of these small species bear a close resemblance to bumblebees and doubtless benefit by the similarity.

The caterpillars are large, fleshy, and usually smooth-bodied. They have the habit of rearing up the front end with the head bent down, that, indeed, reminds one of the attitude of the sphinx. Most of the caterpillars have a strong horn near the rear end of the abdomen, and thus are often called "hornworms." **87**

The American four horned sphinx (Ceratomia amyntor) is exceptional in having horns on the thorax. Many sphinx caterpillars have slanting lines or spots along the sides that act as camouflage, breaking up their outlines and resembling the parallel veins of leaves. It is surprising how difficult it is to distinguish a big, three- or four-inch-long larva from foliage, obvious though it may look when isolated. Some larvae, such as the European elephant hawk (Deilephila elpenor), have a pair of big, realistic-looking eyespots on the thorax, which may well deter predators.

The larvae usually enter the ground to pupate in a cell, rarely in a loose cocoon. The pupae are mostly plain brown, although some have spots. In one group the tongue case of the pupa, where the proboscis is developing, is free at one end and is shaped like a jug handle.

Not many sphingids are harmful to man's interests; for most of the species either feed on plants of little economic importance or else never become abundant. However, North American tobacco and tomato hornworms of the genus Manduca can be serious pests. The most important controlling agents are parasitic wasps and flies. It is common to see a large sphinx caterpillar bearing cocoons formed by larvae of a parasitic wasp that have developed within and emerged from their shrunken host.

▲ Hummingbird Moth, Hemaris thysbe

Owlet Moths and Others

Family Noctuidae

This family, the largest in the order, contains thousands of species, ranging from half-inch midgets to giants with wing expanses of more than twelve inches. Most are plant-eaters, the majority feeding on foliage, but others eat buds, flowers, fruits, seeds, tender shoots, stems, or roots. Sizable groups are scavengers in dead leaves and the mold of the forest floor. Needless to say, some are among the worst agricultural pests, especially to field and garden crops. A very few are somewhat beneficial to man, feeding on scale insects, but one of these eats the valuable lac insect, our source of shellac. A few are "cannibals" on other caterpillars. The adults of one group puncture valuable soft fruits and suck the juice; in Asia, one species is known to suck blood from humans, the only lepidopteran to do this.

The majority of the moths are relatively dull colored, usually gray and brown, but there are also many with bright colors and bold patterns. A few are day-fliers and visit flowers, but the majority spend the day on bark or in foliage where their cryptic appearance enables them to avoid notice. The European merveille-du-jour *(Griposia aprilina)* is one of many that have evolved a strong resemblance to the lichens on treetrunks where they rest. Some are very flat and hide in unbelieveably thin cracks or under loose bark.

▲ Underwing Moth, *Catocala*

Underwing moths, mostly of the genus *Catocala,* are classic examples of "flash coloration": the sudden, startling exposure of bold patterns and bright colors when the moth is disturbed. The moth shows only its cryptic forewings as it rests on a matching surface. The hindwings of various species are white, light blue, yellow, orange, or red, banded with black. The exposure of these when the moth leaps into flight is indeed startling; so is their sudden disappearance when the moth dodges behind another treetrunk and lands on it, again with only the cryptic forewings showing. The underwings are great favorites with collectors who not only catch them at lights, but "sugar" for them with baits of fermenting fruits, molasses, and beer. North America has more *Catocala* than the rest of the world, including the white underwing *(Catocala relicta),* which is beautifully camouflaged on white-birch trunks. Some of the

very distinctive *Catocala* are in Europe and Asia. Large species have wing expanses up to four inches. The European *C. fraxini* has pale blue hindwings. The Asian *Othreis* and *Phyllodes* have much the same flash colorations and habits. *Catocala* larvae are unusually good mimics of bark and twigs. Some can jump several inches when disturbed.

The largest noctuids are the *Thysania* of tropical America, expanding up to twelve inches. The closely related black witch (*Erebus odorata*) sometimes flies northward, even to Canada, in the autumn, causing quite a sensation when one flies into a house. Many southern and tropical noctuids as well as some other moths and butterflies, have this habit of working north- **91**

◀ Merveille-du-jour, Europe

ward in summer or autumn. The notorious *Heliothis zea,* variously called bollworm, corn earworm, or tomato fruitworm depending on which crop it attacks, is one of these. A closely related species does the same thing in Europe and northern Africa. Northward flights of millions of the tropical American cotton leafworm *(Alabama argillacea)* occur regularly. Another very harmful noctuid is the armyworm *(Pseudaletia unipuncta).* The striped larvae feed on grasses and grain crops. When they have built up large populations they stage mass marches across country, even in daytime, leaving a trail of devastated crops behind.

Some of the most harmful noctuid larvae are the so-called "cutworms," mostly rather smooth, dull-colored caterpillars that hide during the day and crawl forth at night to feed on seedlings and young, tender plants. A cutworm often eats only a part of the plant that it cuts off. Some climbing species take over where the ground-level ones left off. They are, of course, anathema to gardeners and farmers.

While the majority of noctuids are rather dull colored there are many striking exceptions. The American pink star moth *(Derrima stellata)* and primrose moth *(Rhodophora florida),* colored pink and yellow, are members of an appearance-group of several moth families that rest in matching flowers. The very beautiful wood nymphs *(Eudryas)* have most curious, balloon-like masses of hair on their forelegs, which they hold outstretched when resting. Their caterpillars, too, which are found on grape, are boldly and disruptively colored with black, white, and red.

The noctuids and related families have complex tympanic hearing organs on the last segment of the thorax. With these they can hear the very high-pitched "supersonic" squeaks made by bats as a method of guiding themselves. On hearing a bat the moths are able to take evasive action. **93**

◀ Black Witch

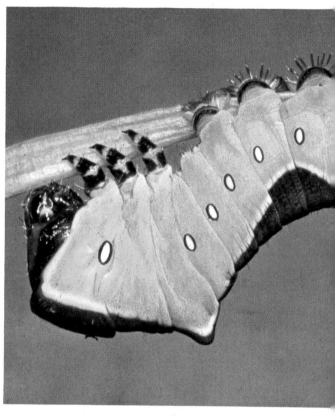

Prominent Moths

Family Notodontidae

The prominents are a sizable, worldwide family, belonging to the great noctuoid complex. The moths are on the whole undistinguished, most being cryptically patterned in grays and browns. Some, however, have bright colors or unusual patterns, sometimes disruptive, but sometimes aposematic in the case of species protected by chemical secretions. The larvae, however, have many extraordinary features.

A peculiar feature of many genera is the evolutionary loss of

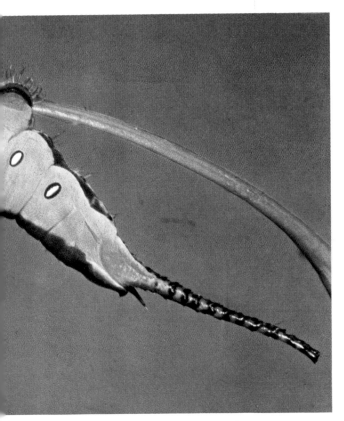

the last pair of abdominal prolegs as functional legs. Many larvae are chemically well protected and are able to squirt highly irritative formic acid from a gland beneath the thorax. This is most extreme in the curious puss moth caterpillars of the genus *Cerura* (and *Dicranura*) in which these legs have become a pair of long, slender whiplashes. When disturbed, the caterpillar elongates these and waves them about violently. At the same time it arches up its head and thorax, sometimes exposing a pair of eyelike tubercles. Since it has highly contrasting color patches as well, an aroused puss moth caterpillar is thoroughly protected and advertises the fact unmistakably.

95

▲ Puss Moth larva, *Cerura vinula,* Austria

In other types the larvae often have large humps or protuberances on a number of segments, which break up their outlines so they look like anything but caterpillars. These larvae also have the last pair of prolegs more or less aborted, and often have bold patches of green and brown or tan that do still more to break up their outlines. Many of them adopt contorted positions and look so much like twisted bits of dead leaves that even experienced observers, let alone birds, overlook them. The disguise is greatly enhanced by the habit many larvae have of eating out part of a leaf and then resting in that space. The green elm leaf caterpillar *(Nerice bidentata)* is a good example of this, having a set of toothlike tubercles along its back that match the teeth on the edge of an elm leaf. The leaf-green *Oligocentria lignicolor* has a big hump and areas of pale, dead-leaf brown.

Still another type of larva is boldly marked with contrasting black and yellow or white stripes, sometimes with a red or orange head. These larvae also have acid-squirting glands beneath the thorax. When disturbed they often raise both the front and rear ends sharply in a warning signal, and squirt acid at the disturber. In some species, such as those of the genus *Datana,* the larvae are sociable, so that the warning is greatly enhanced

▲ *O. lignicolor*

▲ Defense pose, *Datana ministra*

by the number of larvae doing it simultaneously. Some of these, *Datana ministra* and *D. integerrima,* are of economic importance, defoliating apple and oak and feeding on walnut and hickory.

Some of the adult moths have their own unusual protective appearances, involving disruptive color patches, unusual tufts of hair or scales, and peculiar resting positions. The European *Pterostoma palpina* rests out in broad daylight on the broken end of a twig or weed stem, looking like the broken end. One was noted spending over six hours thus in an Oxford garden, and until a bird tried to land on the end of the stem, it was perfectly undisturbed. Adults of the white-S prominent and of *Datana* have dark patches on the front end that look like the cavity at the end of a broken stem. The adults of the genus *Schizura* roll the dull, streaky wings around the abdomen and rest with this cylinder projecting outward from a branch, look-

98 ing like a stub or twig.

Foresters

Family Agaristidae

The agaristids are a small but worldwide family of moths of the general noctuoid complex that interests naturalists and scientists for a number of reasons. The moths are very active and fast flying, visiting flowers during the daytime. Typically they have bold, striking patterns of black, spotted or banded with white, yellow, pale blue, or scarlet, and are always conspicuous. There is reason to suspect that they are somehow protected by toxins or impalatability (birds seem to leave them alone), but no analyses have shown this. The caterpillars, too, are definitely aposematic-looking, banded with white, black, and red. They feed in the open. Those of the North American eight spotted forester *(Alypia octomaculata)* feed on ivy and grape, and are occasional pests. Perhaps the most unusual species are the Australian whistling moths of the genus *Hecatesia* in which the males have a structure on each forewing they use to make a whistling noise when disturbed. Like the supersonic noises of the arctiids this may be some sort of aposematic signal of impalatability, but it is more likely a courtship performance.

Tiger Moths and Woolly Bears

Family Arctiidae

This interesting family is large and worldwide. They are most abundant in tropical regions, but at least one species extends far into the "high" arctic. Many of the moths are brightly, even brilliantly, colored and patterned. Enough of them have been shown to harbor toxins to lead to the belief that most are chemically protected. The same is true of the caterpillars, many of which are also brightly colored and patterned. Many have exceedingly long, dense hairs, and are called woolly bears. Few species are economically important, although some feed on weed plants.

The species known as tiger moths have boldly patterned wings, the hindwings often bright with black and scarlet, orange, yellow, or white. On each side of the front of the thorax is an opening from which an attacked moth bubbles a toxic or distasteful liquid. More than one toxin has been identified in the European garden tiger *(Arctia caja)* including histamines, alkaloids, and traces of cardenolide heart poisons. Some arctiids fall over on their sides when roughly treated, "playing possum" and exposing bright abdominal colors. Some woolly bear caterpillars do the same, curling into a tight ring and presenting only a mass of long hairs or spines.

The moths' excellent tympanic hearing organs are sensitive to the supersonic sounds of the sonar hunting mechanism of bats, and enable the moths to take evasive actions. In addition the moths can produce supersonic sounds, which may both "jam" the bats' hearing and also serve as aposematic warning signals. The moths of the related family Ctenuchidae also do this. In fact, they and the arctiids are at the peak of aposematism with highly protective chemicals; distinctive colors, patterns, and behavior;

▲ Cinnabar Moth, Europe ▼ Jersey Tiger Moth, Spain

special defensive displays; and sonic organs for both hearing and warning.

In some arctiids the wing patterns are highly disruptive, that is, they break up the outline of the moth into two or more distinct areas, making it look like anything but a moth. Species of the North American genus *Haploa* are noted for this. The worldwide genus *Utetheisa,* consisting of a few, essentially tropical day-flying species, has characteristic brightly colored and dotted patterns. Although fragile, the African crimson speckled *(U. pulchella)* stages enormous northward migrations across Europe and even far out to sea.

The North American summer and fall webworms of the genus *Hyphantria* are white moths that live gregariously as larvae in large, spreading silk webs, well out on the branches of trees. They disfigure and damage valuable trees such as hickory and apple. They are often erroneously called "tent caterpillars" *(Malacosoma* of the Lasiocampidae). The fall species *(H. cunea)* is proving something of a pest in Europe, where it was introduced.

Many arctiid larvae, as well as the adults, are highly aposematic, such as the orange-and-black larvae of the European cinnabar moth *(Hypocrita jacobeae).* The larvae feed on ragwort, a troublesome weed, and are therefore somewhat beneficial. The striking orange, black, and white larvae of the American milkweed tussock *(Euchaetias egle)* are undoubtedly protected and highly aposematic, and also somewhat sociable. The familiar orange-red and black banded woolly bear *(Isia isabella)* is often seen, particularly in autumn, looking for winter quarters. An old country superstition says that long black ends on woolly bears foretell a long winter. The European and American garden tiger caterpillars are very striking, with long, frosted black hairs **102** above and brown to chestnut ones below.

▲ Defense pose, Salt Marsh Moth, *Estigmene acraea* ▼ *Utetheisa bella*, Florida

▲ Wasp-mimic, Jamaica

Ctenuchids

Family Ctenuchidae

The ctenuchids are a worldwide family of about two thousand species, especially abundant in the tropics, with a few species ranging northward into Canada. They are chiefly day-flying flower-visitors, and are noted for their defensive adaptations. Protected by high levels of heart poisons and irritant or toxic histamines in their blood, most have bold, brightly colored, aposematic appearances and actions. Often they mimic wasps, toxic lycid beetles, or other protected moths. Some wasp mimics are very convincing not only in appearance, but in behavior, pretending to sting with an imitation stinger at the end of the abdomen. Some have special defense postures that show off their distinctive features; others make sounds in audible ranges and in the supersonic ranges used by bats. Some have special scent secretions repulsive to other animals but perhaps functioning as sex attractants to their own species. The polka dot moth *(Syntomeida epilais)* can be a pest on oleander; its orange-and-black larvae and orange pupae are also strikingly aposematic.

▲ Gypsy Moth caterpillar

Tussock Moths and Others

Family Lymantriidae

The moths of this small but worldwide family are mostly broad winged and dull colored, and do not feed. The males typically have sensitive, plumy antennae and fly actively seeking females. In some females the wings are entirely absent, in others they are reduced or little used. The eggs are often laid in masses, covered with the female's abdominal vesture. The female European gold tail *(Euproctis chrysorrhoea)* manages to get her own stinging larval hairs, by way of her cocoon, onto her abdomen and then protects her egg mass with them. The European browntail moth *(Nygmia phaeorrhoea)*, introduced into North America, was a serious pest because of the larval stinging hairs as well as damage to trees, although it has now largely disappeared.

Many of the caterpillars are quite well protected from predators, having projecting ''shaving brush'' tussocks of hair, and often long, thin hair-pencils. Some also have osmeteria, or projecting scent organs with a repellent, protective function. Some also have sharp, barbed hairs that can cause an itching or

▲ White Marked Tussock, U.S.A. ▼ Scarce Vapourer

burning rash. Many have bright blue, red, or yellow markings. Despite these protections, however, many lymantriid caterpillars are eaten by birds such as the North American cuckoos and catbird.

The lymantriids include a disproportionate number of bad pests on trees. The infamous European gypsy moth *(Porthetria dispar)*, introduced into North America, has defied controls and is going stronger than ever, seriously damaging forest, orchard, and shade trees. It has reached Texas, Canada, and Minnesota. The females scarcely, if ever, fly; the species is spread by vehicles and by tiny larvae that hang from threads and are blown by the wind. Quarantine and barrier zones have not been effective, and the use of such insecticides as DDT has been prohibited because of their enormous and long-lasting ecologi- **106** cal damage. Other controls attempted include importation of

parasitic wasps, flies, and predatory insects, and distribution of fungi, and bacterial and virus diseases. Also, the males have been trapped and sterile males released to mate with females. All of these do some good, but none is adequate.

In Europe, especially in Germany, the black arches, or nun, moth (Lymantria monacha) is a forest pest. Several North American species of Orgyia and Hemerocampa occasionally damage forests, particularly in the West. The white marked tussock (Hemerocampa leucostigma) is injurious to shade trees in polluted, dirty cities. The wingless females on their own cocoons await the males, and then lay their eggs there. One interesting lymantriid (Byrdia rossii) has no economic importance and lives in even the bleakest, far arctic lands where its big, very hairy caterpillars can be seen scurrying from one three-inch-high willow to another. **107**

▲ Male Gypsy Moth, New Jersey

Skippers and Giant Skippers
Superfamily Hesperoidea and Family Megathymidae

Many people automatically categorize skippers with true butterflies, although skippers are really quite different, in some ways more primitive. But both groups are day-fliers and flower-visitors, and contain many brightly colored members. Butterfly collectors are usually collectors of skippers as well. There are three skipper families: one contains but a single species, the regent skipper *(Euschemon)* of Australia; another is the true skippers *(Hesperiidae)*. The giant skippers *(Megathymidae)* are large, with wing expanses of up to three inches. They also have powerful, heavy bodies, and can fly exceedingly fast. There are perhaps fifty species, centering in Mexico and the southernmost United States. Their plain-looking larvae bore in the pithy stems and leaf bases of yucca (spanish bayonet) and agave (including maguey) plants characteristic of desert and semidesert regions. Some larvae make silken tubes leading away from the plant for several inches, and live and pupate in these. The tubes incorporate much surface dirt, so they are not easily seen. The group was little known until quite recently when it was discovered how to find and rear the larvae, which are often canned for hors d'oeuvres as *gusanos de maguey*.

▲ Giant Skipper, *Agathymus aryxna*

▲ Tropical Checkered Skipper, *Pyrgus syrichtus,* Florida

True Skippers

Family Hesperiidae

The true skippers are a worldwide family of more than three thousand species. The antenna has a thinner end portion beyond the club and is hooked at the tip. Most species are avid flower-visitors, feeding through their long, strong tongue, and are important in cross-pollination. The flight is very fast and direct, with no fluttering. The caterpillars are also quite plain, except for head markings, and have an apparent neck between the head and body. The larvae live in individual nests made by folding and tying parts of leaves or grassblades where they hide by day, only coming out to feed at night. The fully grown larvae usually pupate in the nest, or nearby, in a loose sort of a cocoon. The pupae are plain and unornamented.

One subfamily, Pyrginae, has proportionately broader wings. Males of many species have a fold at the front edge of the forewing containing sexual scent scales. The larvae feed on a variety of broad-leaved plants from herbaceous species to trees. Most of the relatively plain adults are black, brown, or grizzled gray, especially in temperate regions. But in tropical regions, particularly in the New World, many species are red, yellow, and iridescent blues and greens, their brilliant colors almost rivaling the hummingbirds'. Some have long graceful tails on their hindwings. The long tailed skipper (*Urbanus proteus*) is one of the very few agriculturally injurious skippers; its larvae are at times a serious pest on cultivated beans. The larvae of the silver spotted skipper (*Epargyreus clarus*)—a large, powerful

◀ Large Skipper, *Ochldes venatus*, Europe
▼ Silver Spotted Skipper

species widely distributed across the United States and Canada, and southward—feed on many leguminous trees, shrubs, and vines, chiefly on locust and wistaria. The bright yellow larvae each have two large, eyelike, yellow spots on their red heads. The dark, dusky wings of the genus *Erynnis* are prominent in North America, with fewer numbers in the Old World. Some fly very early in the spring, even before most spring butterflies. But Europe and temperate Asia have a large number, far more than the New World, of grizzled skippers (chiefly of the genus *Pyrgus*), which are small species with many fine dark and light markings.

Another subfamily, Hesperiinae, contains the branded skipper, and is a large group with at least some species common **111**

everywhere. The Old World has relatively fewer species than the New World, and they are especially numerous in North America. The larvae mostly feed on grasses and related plants, living and pupating at the bases in crude nests. Few of these skippers are of economic importance. The adults are commonly yellow to orange-brown with dark markings and borders. Males typically have a thin, dark line of sex scales— the "brand"—on the forewings. Some skippers are very small, with wingspreads of about a half-inch, and can be distinguished from small butterflies by their fast, darting flights. They are eager flower-visitors and important pollinators.

The common European *Thymelicus* (or *Adopaea*) *lineola* was imported into Ontario in about 1910. For many years its range slowly extended but it began moving much faster in the 1960's and has now reached the Atlantic coast. The species may prove something of a pest in lawns. (Our superhighways, with their enormous and continuous areas of grass verges, make wonderful pathways for the spread of these and other grass-feeding insects.) The Brazilian skipper *(Calpodes ethlius),* ranging from South America to New York, is large and dark with translucent white spots. Its larvae feed on canna, and can be injurious.

Scarce Swallowtail, *Graphium podalirius*, Spain ▶

Swallowtails and Parnassians

Family Papilionidae

Here belong many of the largest and most beautiful butterflies. Almost everywhere there are some familiar and admired species. The graceful and colorful adults fly strongly, usually in the open, and are avid flower-visitors. Quite a number do not have the swallowtails. Bright colors predominate, with patterns of yellow, white, orange, red, and iridescent blue and green. The six long legs are strong and hold the butterflies while with fast fluttering wings they probe flowers. Often they visit wet areas and sip liquids in large, sociable groups. Many species are definitely chemically protected and involved in mimicries with other butterflies and moths. All have a protective, forked scent organ, the osmeterium.

The caterpillars are varied, and also often brightly colored. The chrysalids are held by a silk girdle around the body as well as the usual cremaster, which is a spine or group of hooks at the end of the abdomen, and silk pad. They are usually cryptic, green or brown, with anterior paired projections.

Parnassians *Subfamily Parnassiinae*

The distinctive parnassians are tailless, thinly scaled, and usually white or gray with dark markings. Often they have one or more red, black, and white spots or eyespots. They are essentially butterflies of mountainous regions, ranging from Spain across Europe to Asia, and in western North America. Some species of the central Asian mountains are particularly magnificent and very rare, and are highly prized by collectors. The foodplants of the parnassians are stonecrops (*Sedum*) and hens-and-chickens (*Sempervivum*). During mating the male deposits a seal, the *sphragis*, on the abdomen of the female that prevents further matings. The rather hairy caterpillars live in individual webs and make a slight cocoon for pupation.

The festoons (*Zerynthia, Thais,* etc.) of Europe and Asia are yellow with dazzling patterns of black and red zigzags. Their caterpillars feed on the highly toxic aristolochia plant, so that they are undoubtedly chemically protected.

True Swallowtails *Subfamily Papilioninae*

Despite their common name, many in this highly varied group lack tails on the hindwings. They differ widely in size, color, caterpillars, foodplants, means of protection, habits, and flights. Some species are common over large areas; others are very rare and local. They are composed of three main groups: the aristolochia, fluted swallowtails, and kite swallowtails. There are also "splinter groups," which represent small, separate twigs on the family tree.

Perhaps the most unusual of the "splinter groups" are the relatively tiny *Lamproptera* of southern Asia, which have nearly transparent forewings and very long, pointed tails. The striking, iridescent green *Teinopalpus,* and the unusual *Armandia* live in forested mountainous regions of southern Asia. *Armandia* has narrowly zebra-striped wings, with an enormous eyespot and three tails on each hindwing. The rather dull brown-and-black *Baronia,* of only certain high mountains in Mexico, looks like anything but a swallowtail. It is an ancient relic that has somehow managed to survive in a very small area.

Birdwing Butterflies

These are justly the most glamorous of all butterflies, as well as the largest. These butterflies (*Ornithoptera, Troides,* and *Trogonoptera*) range from India through the Australasian region. The males are black with large iridescent areas of blue, green, or yellow. The females, which are larger (up to eleven inches expanse), have many white and black patterns and little, if any, iridescence, except in *Trogonoptera*. The butterflies are very high-flying, seldom approaching the ground. The first female specimen of the magnificent Solomon Islands *Ornithoptera victoriae,* taken about 1884, was, in fact, brought down by a shotgun. They are aristolochia feeders, and thus inedible. The big black caterpillars have rows of pointed, often brightly colored tubercles. Collectors have paid very high prices for some of the rarities, threatening their extinction. The Australian government has wisely protected them by laws forbidding collecting or trafficking in them.

▲ Raja Brooke's Birdwing, *Trogonoptera brookiana*

Aristolochia Swallowtails

The Aristolochiaceae, or birthworts, is a small, worldwide family of plants containing some quite toxic substances. Insects that can safely eat these plants and store the toxins in their bodies, are thereby themselves rendered inedible. Prominent among these protected insects are the great birdwings. The butterflies tend to be distinctively aposematic and shunned by predators. Most are brightly colored with black, iridescent blues or greens, and orange or red spots or patches. Predictably, they are deeply involved in a riot of both Batesian and Müllerian mimicry with butterflies and moths of many families, especially in the New World. The North American pipevine swallowtail *(Battus philenor)* is mimicked by a dark female variety of the yellow-and-black tiger swallowtail *(Papilio glaucus)*, the spicebush swallowtail, *(P. troilus)*, the red spotted purple *(Limenitis astyanax)*, and the females of the Diana fritillary *(Speyeria diana)*.

Kite Swallowtails

The kites are a large, worldwide group containing many species of great interest and beauty. Kites typically have a pair of very long, graceful tails, and light-colored wings crossed by narrow black lines, but many of the species lack tails and have very different patterns. The very widely distributed *Graphium sarpedon* of the Indo-Australian region is black, with a wide, pale green or blue band across the wings. The chrysalids have a horn on the thorax. *G. podalirius* can be found in Europe and North Africa; in North America is the pale green pawpaw swallowtail *(G. marcellus)* with a number of seasonal varieties. Other species fly in New World tropics and in Asia to Australia. The caterpillars feed in a variety of trees and shrubs, including some cultivated fruit trees. The butterflies may often be seen alighting **116** in considerable numbers on wet earth.

▲ *Lamproptera curius*, Hong Kong

Fluted Swallowtails

Here belong many of the most familiar swallowtails the world over. The inner margin of each hindwing is fluted but not folded to include a mass of scent scales. The chief European species, *Papilio machaon,* is largely yellow, with dark borders, a blue band on the hindwing, and an orange-and-black "target" eyespot. In other European, Asian, and North American members of its group, such as the widespread black swallowtail *(P. polyxenes),* the yellow areas are narrower or are reduced to a row of spots. Some large tropical species have broad bands of color crossing the black wings—yellow bands in the magnificent *P. homerus* of Jamaica and blue in the astonishing *P. ulysses* of Australasia. The larvae feed on umbelliferae such as carrot, parsley, and fennel; they are boldly cross-banded with yellow to orange osmeteria that give off pungent butyric acid compounds. The fleshy, smooth caterpillars of other groups are green or brown and often have startlingly realistic eyespots on

▲ Black Swallowtail, *P. polyxnes,* North America

the body and various disruptive markings. The American *P. cresphontes* and *P. andraemon* are citrus-tree pests.

Dardanus Swallowtails

This African swallowtail *(Papilio dardanus)* is the most famous and complicated Batesian mimic of protected butterflies. All males and "normal" females are long-tailed and creamy yellow with bold black markings. But in certain regions the females of *dardanus* have evolved excellent mimicries of common, highly protected, danaid butterflies that enjoy comparative immunity from predators. One of these model species is the tailless, white-on-black *Amauris niavius*. Another is the also tailless, orange-brown *Danaus chrysippus*, widespread in Africa and Asia. Their mimicry is so good that the swallowtails were for long believed to be danaids. They even mimic the flight habits of their models. *P. dardanus* has recently been the subject of a great amount of genetic and geographic research, and has thus contributed to our understanding of evolutionary processes. **119**

▲ European Swallowtail, *P. machaon*

Whites and Sulphurs

Family Pieridae

These butterflies constitute a large family with members almost everywhere, even in the extreme arctic. The name "butterfly" was probably first inspired by a yellow European species. Except for a few mimetic species, nearly all are white, yellow, or orange. Alone among butterflies, the pierids derive their pigments from the common excretory waste, uric acid. Structural iridescence is rare. Like the swallowtails, but unlike most other butterflies, the adults of both sexes have fully developed, functional forelegs. In some genera the males have patches of sexual scent scales on the wings. A few groups of the New World tropics mimic some of the highly protected, aposematic heliconiid, ithomiid, and papilionid butterflies; the females are the chief mimics. In some whites and giant sulphurs there is at least a partial genuine protection by alkaloids and mustard compounds derived from the foodplants. Many species are very fast fliers, and some are migrants.

Pierid eggs are usually long and spindle-shaped, and are placed on end. The caterpillars are generally plain and cryptic, green to yellow with lines along the sides and sometimes cross bands or spots. They are often downy, covered with a short pile of close-set hairs. None are very hairy or have prominent horns or tubercles. A few are harmful to agriculture. The chrysalids are held by a silk girdle as well as by the cremaster, and in all but one genus they have a single horn protruding forward from the head. In some genera the wing cases are greatly expanded. Most of the chrysalids are cryptic, green or brown.

Clouded Yellows and Sulphurs

Some of the most familiar butterflies are of the genus *Colias,* found in the North Temperate Zone of Europe, Asia, and North America, with outliers in Africa and tropical America. Some extend far into the arctic, where one, *Colias hecla,* lives at the northernmost limits of land in Greenland and Ellesmere Island. In that rigorous climate, with its very short growing season, these butterflies need two years to complete a single growth cycle. Some Siberian species are particularly magnificent: yellow to orange and scarlet, and an odd pale blue one. Most

Colias are strong, fast fliers, and a South American species stages large migratory flights. Charles Darwin recorded one "like a snowstorm" out to sea from Argentina in 1842. It was recently discovered, through ultraviolet photography, that the males of many species have brilliant ultraviolet reflections from their wings. The reflections are visible to the butterflies but above the range of human vision, and undoubtedly play an important part in courtship behavior.

Both the downy caterpillars and the chrysalids are green and cryptic. The abundant North American alfalfa butterfly *(Colias eurytheme)*, a bright orange-and-black species, is sometimes a pest. Its close relative, the clouded sulphur, or mud-puddle butterfly *(Colias philodice)*, is a clover-feeder. As in many *Colias* the young, recently emerged males gather in swarms on wet ground to drink heartily before scattering to seek mates.

121

▲ Sulphurs, *Terias*, on wet earth

Giant Sulphurs

Many of the large sulphurs of the tropical genera *Catopsilia* and *Phoebis* are abundant and well known for their mass migratory flights, which sometimes include many millions of individuals. The chief species are *Catopsilia florella* in Africa, *C. crocale* in the Orient, and *Phoebis eubule* in the New World. The American *Phoebis eubule* sometimes flies northward in numbers in autumn and is the only species to travel far distances away from tropical or subtropical regions. Most species are white or yellow, but some are brilliant orange. *Phoebis avellanada* of Cuba, yellow and orange with scarlet markings, is one of the world's most striking butterflies. The adults, generally fast, powerful fliers, are consistent flower-visitors, and often form large swarms to sip water along stream banks and at the edges of puddles. The caterpillars feed on various leguminous plants such as locusts and mimosas. The chrysalids have enormously expanded wing cases.

Orange Tips

The orange tips are essentially a Northern Hemisphere group with the majority of species in Europe and North America, others in north Africa and the Near East, and one offshoot each in Asia and South America. The butterflies are white or yellow; many have orange patches at the tips of the forewings, and many are cryptically marked beneath with greenish marbling or patches. A surprising number do very well in desert and semidesert regions; and in Europe and North America at least one species reaches the Arctic Circle. The cryptic green larvae feed on herbaceous plants, chiefly of the mustard family. The chrysalids, also cryptic, often have extremely long, projecting horns on the head, which make them look like spines along a twig. The most widespread European species is *Anthocharis cardamines*; in western North America *A. sara* ranges widely, with considerable local and geographic variation.

Cabbage Butterflies

Few butterflies are harmful to man's interests, but the European cabbage butterfly, or small white *(Pieris rapae)* is a pest wherever it flies. Originally a native of Europe and temperate Asia, it was introduced into North America in about 1860 and soon
spread over most of the continent. It reached New Zealand in

1930 and Australia in 1939. The highly cryptic, green larvae are destructive to cabbage and many related plants, including mustard, cauliflower, and Brussels sprouts. They are also pests on nasturtium (which contains the same essential oil as cabbage) and mignonette. Control by poison sprays is being phased out in favor of control by parasitic wasps; one very useful wasp specializes on the chrysalids, others on the larvae. In Europe the large white *(Pieris brassicae)* is also a pest; so far it does not seem to have emigrated elsewhere.

▲ Orange Tip, *Anthocharis cardamines*

Metalmarks

Family Riodinidae

The great majority of these small butterflies live in New World tropics. There they show an incredible variety, from dull brown species to iridescent blue and green ones. Some have partly transparent wings; some have one or two long tails on the hindwings. Many are involved in mimicry complexes with moths and other butterflies. Europe has only one species, North America about twenty, and the rest of the world a scattering. Some of the temperate-zone species, such as those of the genus *Lephelisca,* have a series of tiny, metallic-looking dots on the wings—hence the name "metalmarks." The front legs of males are reduced in size; the other two pairs (and all legs of the females) are normal. In some species the adults have a curious habit of landing abruptly from flight on the underside of a leaf.

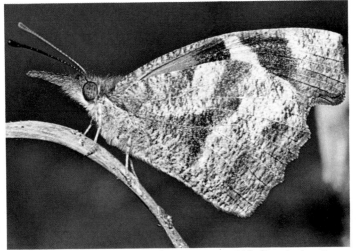

▲ *Libytheana bachmanii*

Snout Butterflies

Family Libytheidae

The snout butterflies are a most peculiar little group: they are an almost worldwide family of only about ten species, all of which look very much alike. The palpi, much longer than those of any other butterflies and most moths, project forward, giving the family its common name. The front legs of males are reduced, those of females normal, much as in the metalmarks and lycaenids. The adults are strong, fast fliers. On rare and unpredictable occasions several of the species, including the North American *Libytheana bachmanii* and some from tropical America and Africa, become abundant and stage spectacular mass migrations. An observer in Texas recorded "millions over a front of 250 miles—from 50 miles north of San Antonio to the Rio Grande." In an African migration the butterflies were so dense that a driver had to stop his car, as it was impossible for him to see his way.

125

◀ Metalmarks, *Apodemia mormo*, mating

▲ Spring Azure, *Celastrina argiolus* ▼ Harvester, *Feniseca tarquinius*

Gossamer Winged Butterflies

Family Lycaenidae

This large, worldwide family of small butterflies contains many familiar and beautiful species. Some have unusual and interesting habits and relationships with other animals. There are three main subfamilies: the blues, hairstreaks, and coppers; one peculiar small one, the harvesters; and a number of odd groups. The caterpillars are short and chunky and keep the head down, often out of sight beneath the prothorax. The short, stout pupae are supported by a girdle as well as the cremaster. The forelegs of the adult males are reduced, the females' are normal.

Harvesters *Subfamily Gerydinae*

North America, Africa, and Indo-Australia have representatives of this very small, highly unusual group. The caterpillars are carnivorous, mostly feeding on such small insects as aphids, or plant lice. (One extraordinary Australian species, *Liphyra*, which feeds on ant larvae in ant nests, probably deserves a subfamily to itself.) The chrysalids all bear a surprising resemblance to miniature monkey heads. The North American *Feniseca tarquinius* feeds on the white, woolly aphids of alder.

Blues *Subfamily Plebejinae*

The world's smallest butterfly, with a wing expanse of a half-inch or less, is the pigmy blue *(Brephidium exilis)* of North America; but all of the blues must be reckoned small as butterflies go. Most of the species are blue, but some are brown, and in others the males are blue and the females brown. The undersides are generally pale, with transverse rows of fine, dark marks and a row of orange spots at the outer margin that may also occur on the upper sides. Few of the species are fast fliers, but they can dodge surprisingly well. They are avid flower-visitors, and are often seen sipping at wet earth. There are numerous species almost everywhere in temperate and tropical regions, and even a few in the arctic and on high mountains. Some are among the first butterflies to fly in spring, and some species have three or even more generations annually, particularly in the tropics.

The caterpillars look short and humpbacked due to their habit of carrying the head bent down beneath the thorax. They often **127**

have camouflage markings and a thick covering of short hairs. They feed on a great variety of plants, from herbs to trees. Many have special relationships with ants, and as an adaptation for this have a "honey gland" that opens on the seventh abdominal segment and secretes a sweet liquid that the ants relish greatly. One often sees ants crawling about the larvae, stroking the vicinity of the honey gland and licking the secretion. The larvae gain protection from the presence of the ants, especially against other ants and parasitic flies and wasps. Some, in fact, like the Argus blues *(Aricia),* seem unable to survive without the attendance and stimulation of ants, and must be carried to fresh foodplants conveniently near the ants' nests. Some are dependent on the ants for more than mere protection. Larvae of the large blues *(Maculinea arion)* of Europe and Asia, feed on thyme or gentian until partly grown, when the ants carry the larvae down into the ant nest. There a larva feeds for some weeks on the brood of the ants, and then stays for the winter. In the spring it feeds on more ant larvae, and eventually matures and pupates. The butterfly then crawls out of the ant nest, spreads its wings, and flies away. These species' dependence on ants is an example of symbiosis, or a mutually beneficial relationship.

▲ Argus Blues, *Aricia,* Austria

Hairstreaks *Subfamily Theclinae*

There are hundreds of hairstreaks, chiefly in the temperate and tropical regions. Many have fine, streaky markings on the undersides of the wings and most have fine, hairlike tails on the hindwings. The temperate-zone species are usually rather dull, gray or brown above (some have orange patches) but often have distinctive, bright colors, often green, beneath, and a row of red or orange spots. A few temperate-zone species, and a great many tropical ones, have iridescent blue on the upper sides that may be as brilliant and changeable as that of the famous morphoes (see p. 135). In fact, if these hairstreaks were as large as morphoes they would outshine them in every way. Many of these brilliant species keep the wings closed above the back when resting and are well camouflaged by their cryptic, often green, undersides.

A very noticeable feature is a bright orange-and-black eyespot at the anal angle of the hindwing. This is an attention-getting "target" that attracts birds and lizards. When the predator attacks, however, it gets only the bit of wing membrane, and the butterfly escapes practically unharmed. Many swallowtails and other butterflies have similar eyespot targets and are often seen lacking this part of the wings, evidence of a successful escape.

A peculiar but characteristic habit of many hairstreaks is to stand with the wings above the back, keeping the forewings still but moving the hindwings alternately forward and back. Perhaps this disperses the aroma from scent scales, which many males have in patches on the forewings.

Male hairstreaks often take up a perch on a leaf, to which they consistently return and from which they dash out to intercept passing females or chase away other males. Many species whose caterpillars feed on tree foliage spend much of their time high in the forest canopy. In general the adults are eager flower-visitors, but they sometimes visit wet earth to sip. Some visit hummingbird feeders for the sweet syrups.

Hairstreak caterpillars are short and stocky, and like those of other lycaenids, keep the head tucked beneath the prothorax and have a ridge along each side that largely conceals the legs. Their shape and slow motions remind one, in fact, of some slug **129**

Imperial Hairstreak, Australia: Larva attended by ants ▲ Adult ▼

▼ Mistletoe Hairstreak, *Callophrys spinetorum*

caterpillars. Many hairstreak and blue caterpillars have a honey gland on the abdomen that secretes a sweet liquid greatly relished by ants, and this is responsible for the special relationships between the caterpillars and ants. In most cases the ants merely attend the caterpillars on their foodplants, stroke them, and imbibe the honeydew. While doing this the ants will defend the caterpillar from attack by potential predators and parasites. In some cases, however, the relationship is more intimate, with the caterpillars pupating in or near the ant nest, and the ants guarding the pupae.

All lycaenid caterpillars and in particular those of blues and **131**

▼ Banded Hairstreak, *Satyrium falacer*

hairstreaks, show a marked tendency to cannibalism; in fact, people who rear them learn to keep them in separate containers. The harvesters and some others have evolved a habit of eating other insects, as well as those of their own group. In many species the caterpillars specialize in eating flowers, and in some species, in boring into developing fruits. A few, such as the North American *Strymon melinus*, do occasional damage to cultivated plants. The pupae are of the usual short, rounded lycaenid type. In many species, as also in blues and coppers, the pupa has a special pair of ridged structures between two abdominal segments which rubbed together make creaking or rasping sounds. This may somehow act as a signal **132** to ants, but its value is uncertain.

American Coppers, *L. phlaeas americana* ▶

Coppers *Subfamily Lycaeninae*

The coppers are an almost worldwide group of small, usually brilliant butterflies. Many are distinguished by bright coppery colors and sometimes iridescent blue or purple. As in so many butterflies, these colors are not due to pigments but are caused by submicroscopic structures in the scales that refract, or break up, the light and give off only certain wave lengths. In one peculiar North American species, the male is bright, light blue, but the female is brownish. One subspecies of the widespread European and North American *Lycaena phlaeas* occurs as far as the northernmost points of Ellesmere Island and Greenland. New Zealand has some unusual species.

The caterpillars, like those of the other lycaenids, are short, stocky, and often thickly short-haired. Unlike many other members of the family, they have no apparent relationships with ants. They feed inconspicuously on a variety of herbs or shrubby plants. The North American bog copper is said to feed on cranberry. The pupae are short, stocky, and rounded, and are held in place by a silk girdle and pad.

Owl Butterflies

Family Brassolidae

The large, unusual butterflies of the genus *Caligo* are found only in the New World tropics. On the upper sides they are dull brown with some dull, iridescent blue and a band of tawny brown to orange across the wings. Beneath, the wings are crossed with many yellowish lines, and have an enormous, dark-ringed, yellow eyespot on each hindwing. A striking effect is created when the butterfly spreads its wings and exposes these "eyes," and the tendency has long been to say that birds, monkeys, and lizards "think" that the butterfly is an owl. This is putting things much too simply, but certainly the sudden appearance of the pair of eyespots has a deterrent "startle" effect.

The butterflies are strong fliers, chiefly at dusk and in the early morning. They are greatly attracted to fermenting fruit, such as mashed bananas, and are often caught with such baits. They sometimes fly into brightly lighted buildings, such as airports, and hang up for the day. Their caterpillars feed on such broad-leaved plants as banana and heliconia.

▲ Morpho, Brazil

Morphoes and Their Relatives

Family Morphidae

The big, blue morphoes of the New World tropics are among the most famous of butterflies. In some, the wings, particularly of the males, are solid iridescent blue above; in others they are black with broad blue bands. *Morpho rhetenor* and *cypris* are the most brilliantly iridescent, while the pearl morpho (*M. sulkowskii*) is intensively pearl-white. In the wild the butterflies are very wary and strong-flying, and quite difficult to catch. The wings of the big blue species are much used for making such things as trays and lampshades; the specimens thus used are reared in large numbers in Brazil.

Numerous *Morpho* relatives inhabit tropical Asia and Australasia, and are usually separated as the family Amathusiidae. None has the intense blue of the true morphoes, but the species of *Amathusia*, *Stichophthalma*, and *Taenaris* are quite impressive in their own varied ways.

◄ *Caligo*, Brazil

Monarchs and Milkweed Butterflies

Family Danaidae

The North American monarch *(Danaus plexippus)* is deservedly famous. It is the only butterfly that makes regular southward migrations in autumn and northward ones in spring. After two or more generations (each usually lasts four to six weeks) in the north, the butterflies fly south for the winter, some of them gathering along the way in great social sleep-ins. A strong, powerful, and soaring flier, the monarch has crossed the Atlantic and Pacific oceans and colonized in the Azores, the Canary Islands, Australia, and New Zealand.

The family is worldwide. The caterpillars feed mostly on plants of the milkweed family (Asclepiadaceae), from which they accumulate powerful cardenolide heart poisons that carry over into the chrysalids and adults. They are thereby well protected from predators, which soon learn to shun them. Both the caterpillars and adults are highly aposematic with distinctive warning colors and patterns. Not surprisingly, they are key factors in a great many mimetic relationships with many other groups of butterflies (and some moths), ranging from swallowtails to nymphalids. They are often the models for Batesian mimicry by unprotected species. The North American viceroy *(Limenitis archippus),* really a renegade admiral (see p. 152), mimics the monarch. The African swallowtail *(Papilio dardanus,* see p. 119) has female varieties that mimic the golden-brown *Danaus chrysippus* in some regions, and completely different-looking, black-and-white danaids in others. Some Indo-Australian danaids, whitish or greenish with heavily dark veins and borders, are mimicked by various tailless swallowtails, some of which are themselves probably protected. Some females of the nymphalid eggflies *(Hypolimnas)* mimic the golden-brown danaids, but their males are completely different.

Like the adults, danaid caterpillars are boldly aposematic. A common type is banded with contrasting dark and light stripes and has two or three pairs of long, quivering tentacles. The chrysalids are short and stubby; many are green or yellow with bright metallic markings. As usual, the chief "enemies," or controlling agents, are parasitic wasps and flies.

▲ Migrating Monarchs resting ▼ *Danaus hamata*, China

▲ *Mechanitis* laying eggs:

Mimics and Glassy Wings

Family Ithomiidae

A specialty of New World tropics, the ithomiids are highly protected by being distasteful or poisonous. With their close relatives the heliconiids and danaids, they are the most consistently mimetic group. Many of the species have distinctive patterns of yellow, orange-brown, and black. Others are largely transparent, with perhaps a narrow black border and a light spot or two. Flying in the obscure shade of the tropical forests or in the light-dappled forest edges, they are very hard to follow—they disappear and then reappear some distance away. In addition to their Müllerian mimicry partners, the ithomiids are themselves models for Batesian mimicry by whites and sulphurs, nymphalids, metalmarks, and even by **138** members of at least three families of moths.

▲ Glass-wing, *Pteronymia* ▼ *Mechanitis*, Brazil

▲ *Heliconius*, Brazil

Heliconiids

Family Heliconiidae

Although they are a small family, almost limited to the New World tropics, the heliconiids are one of the most interesting groups of butterflies. The key to understanding their many peculiarities lies in the fact that as larvae they feed on various species of passion-flower vines, the Passifloraceae, and from these they either absorb, or synthesize, or both, toxic or distasteful substances. This makes them highly protected against such predators as birds, lizards, and monkeys. One or two attempts at eating a heliconiid will teach an inexperienced predator to shun anything that looks like it. The heliconiids are protected even further, for they are tough and rubbery and can often recover from a pinch that would kill an ordinary butterfly. Most of them are slow and bold in flight almost as though they were daring a bird to attack them. They often gather in groups to hang up together for the night, the same individuals coming together

Zebra, Florida ▶

night after night for weeks at a time. The defensive effect of the group is greater than that of the individuals separately.

The heliconiids and the ithomiids, which are similarly protected, are two key groups in much of the mimicry for which the New World tropical region is famous. They are mimicked by a number of families, themselves perfectly edible, including swallowtails, sulphurs, metalmarks, nymphalids, satyrs, and several families of moths. These gain protection from their Batesian mimicry. But much more striking are the ways in which protected ithomiids, heliconiids, danaids, and some other butterflies have evolved Müllerian mimicries of each other. The resemblances are so close that butterflies that we now know belong to different families were originally thought to be members even of the same genus. Conversely, butterflies now known to be merely different forms, or subspecies, of a single species were originally named as separate species. In one region two or more species may be black with a large red patch on the forewing, elsewhere they may both have added a bright yellow bar on the hindwing, and in another region the hindwing may have bold red markings.

Very few heliconiids are found away from strictly tropical regions. One, the zebra *(Heliconius charitonius),* is common in southern Florida. Another, the gulf fritillary *(Agraulis vanillae),* ranges northward to North Carolina and California. Although presumably protected by its larval passion-flower diet, it is a fast-flying butterfly with brilliant silvery markings on the underside of the hindwings.

Satyrs and Wood Nymphs

Family Satyridae

In Greek mythology the satyrs were a group of minor woodland deities. Nearly all satyrid butterflies, however, feed on grasses and related plants, so that while many satyrids do live around the edges of woods and in forest clearings, many more live in meadows and grasslands. There are satyrs from the northernmost arctic lands and high mountaintops to lush tropical canopy forests. Most are somewhat cryptically colored and patterned, with at least some eyespots near the wing margins. The caterpillars taper sharply at each end, the rear end being forked. The head often has a pair of short horns. The plain chrysalids are held by the cremaster, sometimes in a cocoonlike covering. The adults seldom go far from vegetative cover into which they can dodge if threatened. They will then fly erratically through even thick vegetation, or drop down and fold the wings above the back. Practically all satyrids are true "stay-at-homes"; an individual seldom gets more than a short distance from where it developed. As a result, many of the species tend to form small, inbreeding colonies.

▲ Meadow Brown, England

▲ Marbled White, *Melanargia galathea*

Europe has an especially large number of satyrids, which is the most numerous family of butterflies on that continent. Many of these, such as the grayling *(Hipparchia semele)* and the great banded grayling *(Brintesia circe)*, are quite noticeable in flight. They can, however, camouflage themselves almost perfectly by dropping to the ground and folding their wings flat above the back, with the forewings inside the hindwings. They may even lean to one side and thus avoid casting a broad shadow. The much smaller ringlets, of the genus *Coenonympha*, which occurs across Europe, Asia, and North America, are often a bright ochreous yellow. Like so many other satyrids, they tend to occur in sedentary colonies with many local forms and subspecies. One, *Coenonympha tullia*, occurs from the British Isles across northern Europe, temperate Asia, and all of North America, including a distinctive subspecies in a salt marsh in New Brunswick—an enormous range for such a small butterfly. A

▲ *Brintesia circe*, Spain

very distinctive genus of satyrs of Europe, northern Africa, and Asia is *Melanargia,* the marbled whites. This group never reached North America. There are a few species that are common almost anywhere in grasslands, up to altitudes of perhaps 5,000 feet in mountainous regions. They too have tended to break up into many local forms and geographic subspecies.

The meadow brown *(Maniola jurtina),* widespread in Europe and the British Isles, is an open grasslands butterfly, favoring meadows where the grass is long. It has been the subject of much research on the inheritance of variations, especially regarding its tendency to form local populations that do not interbreed even with close neighbors. Although meadow brown caterpillars feed at night, they can be collected in large numbers if a sort of trawl is dragged across the meadows they inhabit. The adults reared from these specimens are studied regarding their local variations and their heredity.

145

▲ Ringlet, *Coenonympha tullia*

North America has far fewer satyrids than Europe, but most of them show the same characteristics. The wood nymph *(Cercyonis pegala)* flies throughout most of the United States and southern Canada. The southernmost populations of Florida and Georgia are very large, with a large orange patch on each forewing; the eastern Canadian ones lack this patch entirely. An interesting *pegala* subspecies that inhabits white alkali flats in the Nevada desert is heavily suffused with white scales that make it match its peculiar environment.

The pearly eyes and eyed browns of the genus *Lethe* are particularly interesting to students of geographic distribution, for they have survived only in two widely separate regions: eastern Asia and eastern North America. The flight of the adults is fast and erratic, making them difficult to catch. They often alight on treetrunks, ready to dodge when approached.

The most beautiful and unusual group of satyrids is that of the genera *Callitaera* and *Hetaerina* of the tropical American forests. As in the Ithomiidae of the same regions, the wings are largely transparent. The outer parts of the wings, especially of the hindwings, are flushed with pinks or purples, and show at least one of the usual satyrid eyespots. Flying in the dense gloom of a canopy forest, the butterflies look like vague bits of disembodied color, almost impossible to follow.

▲ Purple Emperor

Emperors

Family Apaturidae

This almost worldwide family, often classified with the nymphalids, contains many interesting, fast-flying species. The adults seldom visit flowers, but often seek miscellaneous sources of food such as carrion, manure, rotting and fermenting fruit, the sweet honeydew secretions of aphids, and leaking sap—the more fermented the better. The slender caterpillars taper toward both ends, have one or more pairs of horns on the head, and have the rear end forked, sometimes deeply, much like satyr caterpillars. The European purple emperors *(Apatura ilia* and *iris)* are essentially tree butterflies, whose caterpillars feed on various willows and sallows *(Salix)*. Their wings above are flushed with bright, iridescent blue. They are greatly prized by collectors, but are becoming rare in some regions and deserve protection.

147

◀ *Callitaera macleannia,* Peru

The hackberry butterflies *(Asterocampa)*, mostly North American, are closely related. The caterpillars feed on various hackberry trees *(Celtis)*. The butterflies often fly at dusk, sometimes into the early night. The males are pugnacious in defending their territories; one will assume a head-down position on a treetrunk, dart out to chase any intruders, and then return to the same spot. In the New World tropics the species of *Doxocopa* have the same changeable, iridescent blue sheen on the wings, and share the family habits, including feeding on *Celtis*.

In a different group of the apaturids are such chiefly tropical genera as *Charaxes* and *Polyura* of the Old World and *Anaea*, *Agrias*, and *Prepona* of the New World. Many of these butterflies have one or two sharp tails on each hindwing. *Charaxes* is particularly widespread, with one species entering southern

148 Europe; but most of the species are African and others extend

▲ *Polyura pyrrha pyrrha*, Australia

through Australasia. Many species were rare in collections until it was found that baits of dung and fermenting fruits would lure the adults to where they could be caught in screen traps.

The species of *Anaea* are often called leaf butterflies. They are brightly colored with orange-brown or iridescent blues on the upper sides, but beneath they are excellent leaf mimics. They often alight on a twig or stem, with the wings above the back and the tails of the hindwing against the twig. They are very hard to distinguish in this position, for they look very much like a dead, protruding leaf, and when they fly the sudden flash of the upper sides is disconcerting. The closely related genera *Agrias* and *Prepona* of tropical forests are fast and powerful fliers and have bright reds or iridescent colors. They, too, can seldom be caught except with baited traps, which may have to be hoisted fifty to a hundred feet above the ground.

149

▲ Hackberry Butterfly, *Asterocampa*

▲ Peacock

Brush Footed Butterflies

Family Nymphalidae

This is by far the largest family of butterflies. The front legs of both sexes are very small and brushlike. The caterpillars are usually spiny or bristly and may have prominent horns. The chrysalids may be ornate, brightly colored and patterned, and often have irregular outlines. The adults are mostly eager flower-visitors, but many also feed at fermenting fruits, sap wounds, or carrion.

The peacock *(Inachis io)* is one of the world's most beautiful butterflies. Its colors are created by delicate blendings of pigment and by structural effects. The peacock's range stretches over most of Europe and eastward into temperate Asia. There is a special sound-making apparatus at the wing bases that may deter bats that would attack it during its hibernation, when it hangs in trees. The wings beneath are very plain and dead-leaf brown, providing effective camouflage.

Closely related are the tortoiseshells, bright orange-and-black butterflies with cryptic undersides and angled wings. They include members of the genera *Nymphalis* and *Aglais* of Europe, Asia, and North America. The wings of the familiar mourning cloak, or Camberwell beauty *(Nymphalis antiopa)* are edged with a band of white. Its range extends widely across Europe, Asia, and North America, and south into tropical America. Also related are the anglewings *(Polygonia),* woodland butterflies that are highly cryptic dead-leaf mimics when they fold their wings. The tortoiseshells and anglewings hibernate as adults, crawling into protected spaces or hanging among dead foliage.

▲ Milbert's Tortoiseshell, *Nymphalis milberti*

Admirals

The admirals, of the genus *Limenitis,* are familiar butterflies of the north temperate regions. Both the European white admiral *(L. camilla)* and the American white admiral *(L. arthemis),* as well as *L. populi, L. reducta, L. weidemeyerii,* and *L. lorquini,* have white bands across their dark wings. But the red spotted purple *(L. astyanax)* and the viceroy *(L. archippus)* look entirely different, mimicking the pipevine swallowtail *(Battus philenor)* and the monarch *(Danaus plexippus),* respectively. Although essentially woodland butterflies, feeding as larvae on various trees, particularly willow and poplar, the adults often fly in open areas. They perch on twigs with the wings flat out at the sides, and prefer other sources of food to flowers. The caterpillars have many small tubercles and a pair of long, rough horns on the body, and are cryptically blotched. They hibernate when very small in a specially prepared rolled leaf. The chrysalids are also cryptically marked and shaped, with a large, rounded hump on the back that effectively breaks up their outlines. Some of the species hybridize to form intermediate-looking specimens.

▲ Red Spotted Purple, *Limenitis astyanax*

▲ *Limenitis lorquini,* California ▼ Red Admiral, *Vanessa atalanta*

Silver Spotted Fritillaries

The silver spotted fritillaries of the genus *Speyeria* are almost exclusively North American, with related genera in Europe and Asia. The great spangled fritillary *(S. cybele),* is one of the most common and widespread. There are many species in western North America, some with the spots on the undersides of the wings not silvered. Many geographic subspecies and local forms have evolved, and these often present interesting problems for collectors. The caterpillars have many short, thick spines, and feed on violets and pansies *(Viola),* mostly by night. The strong-flying adults visit flowers ardently.

There are fewer species of the lesser fritillaries *(Boloria),* but the genus ranges from Spain across Europe, Asia, and North America. The silver bordered fritillary *(B. selene)* thus ranges from the Pyrenees to Maryland. Some of the species live in the high arctic, as far north as land animals exist.

▲ Pearl Crescent, *Phyciodes tharos,* North America

▲ Small Silver Bordered Fritillary ▼ Great Spangled Fritillary

In contrast, the variegated fritillary *(Euptoieta claudia)* belongs to a genus that ranges from the United States to the South American Andes. The adults have no silver spotting. The brightly colored caterpillars feed on violets and pansies. The chrysalids are also brightly colored and patterned.

Clicking Butterflies

The clicking butterflies *(genus Hamadryas)*, or "crackers" as they are sometimes called, have been the objects of interest and speculation for a century and a half. They have a special mechanism at the base of each forewing by means of which a loud series of clicks is produced by the males at certain times. The young Charles Darwin was especially intrigued by this phenomenon when he first encountered it in Brazil. It is possible that, as was originally conjectured, this is a "startle" mechanism to confuse possible attackers. But we now know that its primary function is territorial: it is used when a male is defending his territory against an intruder or when a number of males are competing. Sometimes the butterflies click at other animals, such as dogs or even humans. Their colors are finely checkered and mottled grays and blue-grays that match the lichen-covered treetrunks on which they rest with the wings out flat; but they may be genuinely protected, for the larvae feed on plants of the spurge family *(Euphorbiaceae)*, which have toxic or highly irritating secretions or hairs. The chrysalids are extraordinary **156** elongated creatures camouflaged by shape and coloration.

▲ *Hamadryas guatemalena,* El Salvador

Index

Numbers in italic refer to illustrations

Alexander B. Klots, Ph.D., F.R.E.S., is
Emeritus Professor of Biology at the City College of New York and Research Associate in
Entomology of the American Museum of
Natural History. He is the author of several
books, including *A Field Guide to the Butterflies of North America* and *The World of
Butterflies and Moths,* and of many popular,
encyclopedia, and research articles. He has
done entomological field work in North
America (including the Canadian Arctic),
tropical America, and Europe.